Legacy

JOHN PILKINGTON

Copyright © John Pilkington 2020

The right of John Pilkington to be identified as the author of this work has been asserted by him in accordance with the Copyright, Designs and Patents Act, 1988.

First published in 2020 by Sharpe Books.

CONTENTS

Chapters 1 – 20

LEGACY

ONE

I cannot rest until I have told of my Year of Astonishment.

There is a need in people, I find, for certainty. Many seek it in their faith, for which they will fight to their last breath. For myself, having passed my three-score years, I have come now to believe only one thing of certainty, apart from the fact of death which comes to all: that the essence of life is movement. All is in motion: the heavenly spheres, the seasons, the migrating birds, the seas, even the land. Do we not hear of hills rearing up and breaking apart, in the land of the Great Turk? And that our very blood is in flux about our bodies, so that when we expire it ceases to flow? Hence, movement is all; when you stop moving, you begin to die.

By such logic, some might say that in my autumnal years I have condemned myself, living a sedentary life at my late father's house. And yet, who can truly foresee anything? Martin Luther, I heard, foretold that the world would end in the year 1600, and plainly it did not. Certain sages, in the time of Henry VIII, predicted an apocalypse in 1624, and since that year is yet to come, a cautious man might take heed. Myself, I was seldom cautious, or temperate, and lacking in those qualities desirous in a magistrate, it is a wonder I ever found myself appointed to such a position. Away with your puff and pedantry, the younger Robert Belstrang would say – I've no tolerance for such. Mark my alliteration: I could have been a poet, as some fawning flatterer who stood before me once said. I lack the patience, was my reply. And the fine is five shillings.

But those were my days of certainty. And I must come now to my purpose, which is to speak of the upheaval of 1616: my Year of Astonishment.

It began on a chill March day, when at a late hour a visitor arrived at Thirldon, the Belstrang house a short ride west of

Worcester. Childers, having lit candles and departed, returned to my private parlour with news that a neighbour was come, in a pitiable state, asking to see me on a matter of urgency. The neighbour, who lived only four miles away but was seldom seen, was John Jessop, a known recusant; or as some might say, a wretched and impoverished Papist.

'A pitiable state? What do you mean?' I enquired.

'In distress... agitated... forgive me, I'm short on synonyms today,' my steward said. His insolence, in recent years, had come to a point where another master might have thrown him out of service, notwithstanding his age and the fact that he had served my father loyally for many decades. In a somewhat poor humour myself, being in recovery from a mild flux to the head, I assumed my most officious manner.

'You asked him his business, of course.'

'I did, but he declined to favour me with the particulars.'

'Then bid him come in. And have someone bring cakes, and sack.'

'He'll not stay to supper.'

'Do you mean you asked him?'

'It was a question, not a statement.' Childers was at his most tiresome that day; at Thirldon we attributed his demeanour to the damp weather. 'But I will ask, if you wish.' Before I could summon a riposte he left the room.

At first sight of John Jessop, I was taken aback. A man of barely fifty years, he looked older – indeed, his hair had almost whitened since my last, fleeting encounter with him, in Foregate Street a year or so year before; Jessop seldom left his seat at Sackersley. And deep-dyed Papist though he was, despised and shunned by some men of my acquaintance, I pitied him. When I invited him to join me by the fire, he sat down gratefully. He was cold, even from his short journey, which was unsurprising given the condition of his old riding cloak. But his manner owed little to the weather: he was, I perceived, in some torment.

'Forgive me, Justice Belstrang,' he said. 'I've no wish to tax you with my troubles, but I fear you're the only one hereabouts who will listen to me.'

'I am sure you know I'm no longer a Justice,' I said, trying to put the man at ease. 'We've known each other long enough, have we not? Despite the tiresome matter of religion that divides us.'

For a moment he looked quite shocked: religion, far from being in any manner tiresome, was everything to a man like him. He had paid heavily for his faith; those who had seen inside the old, crumbling manor of Sackersley spoke of leaking roofs, furniture and hangings sold off to pay fines, the few remaining servants dressed in threadbare livery, bound by little more than common faith with their master and mistress. Catherine Jessop was never seen: some even said she was dead, and buried secretly in a shroud filled with consecrated earth.

'I have not come to speak of religion,' he said, 'but on a matter of personal need. I'm here as a father, like you, who I'm certain would spare nothing in the pursuit of his child's wellbeing.'

I made no answer; he made me think of my daughter Anne, whom I'd not seen in more than four years. But since he must have meant his only surviving child, a son of about nineteen, I put the thought aside and let him continue, whereupon he reached inside his sleeve and produced a folded paper.

'I received this by carrier today. It was sent from London, where it appears Thomas has been for some months. His mother and I fear something terrible has occurred - will you read it in confidence, and assure me of your keeping private counsel? I believe you're a man of honour, despite the loose reputation you have gained of late, in certain quarters.'

He levelled a gaze at me: not so much imploring me as challenging me - to be true to my word, I assumed. I was wary now, as several thoughts arose in rapid succession. *In primis:* by allowing a Catholic to confide in me, I might lay myself open to charges of collusion. *Secundus:* I recalled that Thomas Jessop was a hothead, a tightly-wound youth whose father had been at pains to keep on a leash, and who might have committed some offence. *Tertius:* the *loose reputation* Jessop spoke of referred to my servant Hester, companion to my late wife, who was assumed by most to be my concubine, though I cared naught for idle gossip. And *quartus:* Jessop's wife was alive after all.

'You risk a great deal, trusting someone like me,' I said

finally.

'No more than would you, if it touched on your child's life,' he said. Then, speaking low: 'I even fear Thomas may be dead.'

'I'll read the letter,' I said. And I did.

My beloved Father

In the great love I bear to you and my dear Mother, I pray you receive these as my last words

to you while I yet live. I mean to make you proud by striking a blow for all those of our

benighted faith who despair of finding Justice and Toleration. By the time you read this letter

you must know the substance of that which I speak of, yet I urge you not to condemn

me but to look inside your heart, and to heed the words of the sage De Talavera.

I beg your forgiveness for my deception in not telling you of my true intent. My only wish is to die in the One True Faith, and to give succour to others in this our time of trial.

Your son in Christ our Redeemer, who commends you to His holy protection,

Thomas Jessop

Sent from Shoe Lane in the ward of Farringdon Without. On the Feast of Simon the Apostle,
1615.

I lowered the letter and handed it back, aware that I was wearing my magistrate's face, which I thought I had shed along with the office. 'The Feast of Simon…?'

'The twenty-eighth of October,' Jessop reminded me. 'And if I might forestall your next question, I do not know why this only came to us now, almost five months late. It's the only message we have received from Thomas since September, when he went away. The deception he refers to is better termed a brazen lie: he told us he was joining a pilgrimage into Wales. We had no inkling he had gone to London, nor do we know the purpose of his visit.'

He fell silent. The letter, in a crabbed and wavering hand, would indeed have given me cause for alarm, were the sender my own offspring. But it smacked of something dark, and now I regretted letting my visitor believe he could count on my discretion. I had not sworn an oath, but...

'Striking a blow - I heartily dislike that. Do you know what he means?'

Jessop indicated that he did not.

'What's this pilgrimage he spoke of?' I asked.

'To the shrine of St Winifred, at Holywell. He begged me for months to give him leave to go there.' He bowed his head. 'I wish to God I'd refused him.'

'Did he say who he intended to travel with?'

'A group of the faithful, though he didn't name them. I remember asking if they meant to keep with tradition, and walk barefoot.'

He fingered the letter, turning it gently in his hands as if it were a holy relic. Then meeting my eye, he said: 'It was an anniversary, that's why I relented.'

'Which anniversary?' I enquired, though I'd no wish to delve any deeper into Popish business.

'It marks ten years since the martyr Edmund Oldcorne went on such a journey,' Jessop said. 'Thomas revered him - I've no need to say more, have I?'

I frowned at that. All England knows of the Jesuit priest Oldcorne, but here in Worcestershire, where he hid for many years in the great Catholic house of Hindlip, his fame is great. As was the crowd at his execution, in the spring of 1606, at Red Hill a mere three miles from where Jessop and I sat. I'm not a man of much sentiment, but the sight of anyone suffering hanging by the neck, drawing of his entrails while yet alive and being chopped in pieces has never been to my taste, whatever his crime.

'No, there's no need to dwell on that,' I said, still frowning. 'Thomas revered him, you say? But he was a child when-'

'He was a witness to martyrdom,' Jessop broke in. 'He was nine years old... most open to impression.'

'And yet, rather than keep the anniversary of that pilgrimage, he went to London instead,' I said, desirous of returning to the matter in hand. 'Do you know if he went alone?'

Jessop shook his head. 'I only know what's in the letter. It came in a small parcel of his private belongings, including a crucifix and his rosary... he would never part willingly with those.'

He gave me a bleak look. 'Should you ask me who sent the package, I do not know. But they knew where to address it.'

The door opened and Childers appeared, carrying a tray with a jug, cups and a dish of sweet cakes. Without looking at either of us he set it down on my small table, made his bow – a sardonic one, I knew – and took his leave. So, with my own hand I poured sack and handed a cup to Jessop, who murmured his thanks before drinking deeply.

'The name your son wrote - De Talavera,' I said. 'Who is that?'

'It means nothing to me,' he answered, wiping his mouth. 'Then, Thomas was become bookish of late... perhaps he read more than was good for him.'

I too drank, in some disquiet. Having digested the substance of my visitor's predicament, I was uncertain what help he thought I could render him. Outside the window dusk had given way to night, and seeing the fire burning low I rose, took up a log and placed it. Jessop appeared to admire the flames that sprang up; then without looking at me he said:

'I cannot go to London to search for him - not even to bring home his body, if that's what must be done. You will know why.'

'I know what the law says,' I replied, after a moment. 'As a Papist you are forbidden from travelling more than five miles from your home-'

'On pain of forfeiting my property,' he finished. 'Which is all I have left.'

'But there's provision,' I argued. 'You can apply for a licence. Given the circumstances, you could lay forth a case...'

'No, I could not.'

He turned to me, and his anguish was plain. 'He waits, and he watches – I speak of our Sheriff, Master Jefferies. Not only would he delight in refusing me license to travel, he would be further delighted were I to attempt to leave in secret. He's most eager to arrest me… can you guess why?' And when I gave a shrug:

'Because the King wants Sackersley, to gift to one of his favourites. He's taken other men's houses, has he not, often on a pretext? Even a loyal Protestant like the great Raleigh lost his country seat…' Jessop's bitterness increased as he spoke. 'What defence does a man like me have? The Crown has been dispossessing our people for eighty years - and I'll wager good Master Jefferies would be well rewarded for clearing the way.'

The cup trembled in his hand, and following my glance he lifted it quickly and drained it. And though I had no special regard for this man, I was moved to pity him as I had upon his first entrance. He spoke the truth, of course, and no more than is common knowledge: King James is most indulgent when it comes to his favoured courtiers, even to the extent of indebting himself.

'But surely there's someone you can call on?' I demanded. 'One who'll go to London and seek for…'

I stopped myself. Surely he did not mean to ask this of me – a protestant, who seldom left his own modest acres? I held his gaze, but he did not waver; he was as desperate as a man could be. This was his purpose in coming to Thirldon, and I should have grasped it sooner.

'You must know that this is a wasted visit, Jessop,' I said then.

'Yet while there is breath, there is hope,' was his reply.

'It's impossible. Some might call it an affront, to ask such a service of me.'

'I've asked nothing of you, sir…'

'Don't dissemble - I see what's in your thoughts.'

'Well - I know no-one else who can go into places I cannot,' Jessop admitted. 'Or speak to people I cannot.'

'Not to your sort of people,' I returned. 'Besides, I've not been at London in years – most of those I knew are dead.'

'Yet you know the city well enough.'

'Twenty-five years ago, perhaps-'

'There is none within ten miles of here with your qualities, Master Belstrang.'

'There are priests you could write to, are there not?' I countered, barely concealing my distaste. 'You'll know the names, and where they might be found.'

A moment passed; but if his hopes of my aiding him were diminishing, he did not show it. 'You know that any such letter would likely be intercepted,' he said. 'I would be writing a death warrant.'

My patience dwindling, I sought a better argument. 'You truly have no inkling of where Thomas might be? No friends, whose company he might seek?'

'Clearly, he lodged somewhere in Shoe Lane. But I know nobody there, and besides that was last October. He could be elsewhere now.'

A new thought struck me. 'He might be overseas, have you not considered that?'

'If you mean he might have gone to somewhere like Douai, or St Omer, or even Rome - believe me, I have considered it,' Jessop answered. 'It was one of my first thoughts, given his youth and his rashness. But his mother and I think it unlikely. He hasn't the means – he had barely a shilling when he left.'

'Unless someone aided him. He would hardly be the first.'

Jessop lowered his gaze; everyone knows that, for many years, zealous young Catholics have been crossing the Channel, intent on training for the priesthood. Finally he spread his hands and said: 'Whatever the reason for his silence, and for the untimely arrival of the package, I must find out the truth. His mother is close to despair...'He looked up suddenly. 'And she does not believe he's dead. She insists that she would know.'

So, there it was. The choice was to stand on my dignity - such as it is - and dismiss the man's suit as improper, not to say impertinent, while expressing due sympathy for his plight. Or to undertake a long, uncomfortable journey on what was almost certainly a fool's errand. It was preposterous, as it was of questionable legality; and besides...

'Your daughter is in London, is she not?' Jessop said, without expression. 'Married, I heard... is that so?'

'To a man I dislike, and who bears the same feeling towards myself,' I retorted, angered by his effrontery. 'And if that is an attempt at blackmail, sir, you'll find I'm immune to such strategies.'

'I know that, Master Justice,' the other said, after a moment. 'As I knew you would hear me out, if nothing more. I came to you as a Christian man, if one of a different kind to yourself. And as a father, who has been put in turmoil by events he did not foresee... perhaps he should have done. I'm but a sinner who prays hourly for guidance, as he prays for the safe return of his child. I can but try any means that may be open to me, while I live.'

He rose to his feet, and set his cup down carefully on the table. 'I'll not trouble you further... I thank you for your hospitality.'

I too stood up, and inclined my head. And though I confess to a feeling of regret, if not of remorse, I had no intention of altering my mind. In silence I accompanied Jessop out to the hallway, whereupon Childers appeared as if by conjuration. Blank-faced, he held out our visitor's hat and riding-gloves. As Jessop took them, he turned to me.

'Our families have been neighbours for centuries,' he said mildly. 'You may recall that Sackersley was built by my grandfather's grandfather, in the time of King Henry the Seventh. He and your forebears would have hunted together, once...'

With a sudden puckering of the brow he broke off as if ashamed of his words, and murmured something barely audible.

To my ears, it sounded like *may God preserve us all*.

TWO

We were a subdued trio at table that evening: Hester and I, and Childers, who took supper with us. Naturally I was obliged to give them an account of my conference with John Jessop. Childers said little, while allowing his dislike of all things Popish to show at intervals. Of Hester's opinion I was uncertain; when it came it was from an unexpected angle, that only a wily skirmisher like she would have chosen.

'Our very lives are shaped by anniversaries, are they not?' She said, by way of casual conversation. 'The King observes several each year...' She began to tell them on her fingers. 'On the twenty-fourth of June, he and the Queen recall the death of the infant Princess Sophia, in 1606. July the twenty-fifth marks the coronation, of course, while on the fifth of August there's always a remembrance sermon, to give thanks for the King's escape from kidnap, back in Scotland. In September comes sad recollection of poor Princess Mary, dead at two years of age – then of course there's even sadder remembrance of the death of our beloved Prince Henry in 1612.' She raised her brows at me. 'Does it strike you as it does me, that all these dates are but celebrations of failure or loss?'

I gave no answer, but busied myself at my roast fowl. Childers, however, chose that moment to put his oar in.

'You have passed over the most memorable failure of all, Mistress Hester. I speak of the Powder Treason of November the fifth, which we celebrate by statute. An event – or rather, the thwarting of it – that's fixed in the fabric of our nation's tale, as it is in perpetual infamy. One in which the King and Queen, the Privy Council, the Bishops and most of Parliament were saved from obliteration, England was saved from Popery and-'

'And a dozen desperate plotters were spared the tedium of living into old age,' I broke in, to quell his prating. 'We've no need for one of your history lessons.'

He bristled, but was ignored. To Hester I said: 'Nor do I need reminders from you. Such dates may be important to the King and Queen, but they mean little to most of the populace.'

'You keep the date of my lady's death sacred,' was her reply. 'As do I.'

'I need no reminder of that, either,' I said, in a tone of reproach.

Hester turned to Lockyer, our serving-man who stood by, and signalled to him to remove her plate. 'I know Catherine Jessop,' she said as he attended her. 'I used to see her at market in Worcester... as gentle and kindly a soul as you could meet.'

Childers and I looked at each other.

'Now I hear she sits by a window most days, like a living statue. It seems most harsh that, living in such dismal circumstances, she should have to bear the loss of her only son.'

'Harsh?' Like an intemperate trout, I rose to her bait. 'No worse than it is for others of her religion. Those stubborn families who keep from church-going condemn themselves - better to attend services they abhor, than bring such penury on their heads. They can confess when they return home, beg forgiveness - tell their rosaries, and whatever else it is they do.'

'This quality you term stubbornness, others might call deep and unwavering faith,' came her reply.

I felt my anger stirring; had I guessed that Hester would take such a position in this matter, I realised, I might have forestalled it. To calm myself, I drained my cup of claret and gestured to Lockyer to refill it.

'If you mean to defend Jessop, you needn't trouble yourself,' I said, when the servant moved off to fill Childers' cup. 'I'm not unsympathetic to the man's plight. Yet what he asked is-'

'Futile?' Hester offered.

'Fantastical,' I corrected her. 'Hunting out a raw youth like Jessop's son is a task for pursuivants, not one like myself.'

'Well, there is that logic,' she replied. 'And you're so hard-pressed here, with all that you do: fishing, and playing at cards – not to forget riding into Worcester to ask after the wine imports. Then, most would say that a former Justice has earned due quietute, in his seventh decade.'

I admit that I was taken aback. Rarely did Hester and I fall to verbal combat; even more rarely did she address me in such a reproachful manner. She had taken up Jessop's case – which of course, was more than Childers could stomach. Fortifying himself with a gulp of wine, he faced her.

'Do you forget that Master Robert would be a Justice yet, had others not connived to have him ousted?' he demanded. 'He was never afraid to cut across the grain, despite what disapproval he attracted– even threats. At least he received the Papist with civility – which is more than the present Justice would have done. And further, I might add...' he swallowed, struggling to curb his choler.

'That I should remember my place here?' Hester finished, meeting his gaze. 'I thank you, Master Childers. I might urge the same upon you.'

'Enough,' I said, more vehemently than I intended. 'I don't care to dwell on what's past - nor to have my supper soured by fruitless discord. The matter's done - I gave my decision, and Jessop understood. He must call upon those of his own persuasion, even the Archpriest if he so wishes... and I'll thank you not to censure me.'

This last was addressed to Hester, who looked pointedly at the table, while Childers grunted and refrained from further argument. Thereafter we sat in silent truce, or more precisely, under ceasefire: the matter lay unresolved, a burr that must be extracted. So, when Hester came to my bedchamber that night I was prepared for another sally. She chose a frontal attack.

'You should go to London,' she said, sitting down on the bed.

'I've said I will not,' I told her, growing weary of the business.

'You know Anne's heartfelt wish is that you visit her at Highgate. Her daughter is four years old, yet you haven't even seen her. After she lost her second child you said you would go – and a pox on her puffed-up husband's disapproval. Those were your words, in exactitude.'

'This is unworthy of you, madam,' I said, fixing my gaze on her.

'It may be so. But in your heart, you know what's true.'

She wore a russet night-gown which had once belonged to her mistress; for a fleeting moment I recalled Margaret in it. Neither of them, whatever dispute might have arisen between us, would stoop to using their charms to sway me, and nor did Hester now. In any case coupling was become rare for us, in our latter years. She reached for my hand, and sitting up in my night-shirt, I took it.

'While you're there you could seek out friends – your old Inns of Court companions,' she said. 'You've talked of them, perhaps more often than you realise. Or do you mean to stay here in soft and balmy Worcester while they die off one by one – until you're ready for your own casket?'

I took a breath, and for argument's sake forced myself to follow her reasoning, as I would do in my magistrate's days. Indeed, now that I turned it about, there was little to keep me from going to London apart from the weather, and a little rain had never troubled Belstrangs. As for seeing Anne and her child: the desire was growing even as we sat in the gloom, our faces lit by the glow of candles.

'And if I did find myself in the capital, I might make casual enquiry as to the whereabouts of the son of John Jessop,' I said, somewhat dryly.

'It would salve your conscience,' Hester said. 'The poor man's visit has troubled you, more than you admit. He's a neighbour, who came to you in desperation.'

'Yet if I did uncover something – unlikely as it seems – it might only serve to compound his grief,' I said. 'At present he and his wife have hope, if little else.'

'If it transpires that their son is dead, or gone abroad, is it not better that they learn of it?' she countered. 'In their place, I would want to know - as would you.'

Plainly I was losing the argument; indeed, I see now that it was already lost. With a sigh, I lifted her hand and kissed it. 'Go to bed now,' I said. 'The room's cold... we'll speak further in the morning.'

She stood up, drawing the gown about her body. 'I'll have the servants make preparations. You should write to your daughter and appraise her of your visit.'

Without waiting to hear me protest, she went swiftly to the door. When she was gone I lay back and pulled up the coverlet, but sleep was slow in coming. Only later did I decide that what

I felt was not foreboding, nor even grim resignation at the thought of a long and tiresome ride. It was anticipation – and something closer to excitement than I had felt in a long while.

Once a decision is taken, I often find, the obstacles to its implementation tend to disappear, as if they were but chimera all along. Childers, however, did his utmost to make himself an obstacle in the few days that followed, to the point where I became desirous of forbearing his company for a time. I'd grown so accustomed to his prating and cavilling, I realised, that I seldom noticed it. So that, on the morning of my departure, when he again expressed dismay at my resolve, I was obliged to use my authority.

'You will hold the keys to the stables and all other outbuildings,' I said, 'but Mistress Hester shall have the house keys, and direction of the kitchens and the buttery.' And when he balked at that: 'Now I require you to ride into Worcester and despatch this letter by fast post-horse to London. Tip the clerk, and the rider if he's near. I'll likely be gone before you return.'

In silence he took the letter, which I had penned to Anne the previous evening. Having seen Hester cheered by my decision, I was surprised to find how eager I was to take to the road.

'Master Justice…' Childers began, at which I stiffened: he only employed that term of address when about to request something. 'Master Justice, if your mind is fixed, at the least take me with you, or one of the servants. You should not undertake such a journey alone.'

I gave him a wry look. 'What, do you think I might fall from my horse? Or be waylaid and robbed, or…'

'A gentleman should be attended, is all I mean.'

'I intend to make speed,' I told him. 'The weather's improving, and I should have two clear days. No other horse at Thirldon can keep up with Leucippus. And of course, I will be armed.'

'Indeed, sir. Nevertheless…' he paused, seeing his remonstrations were futile. Somewhat forlornly, he added: 'May we not ride together as far as Worcester, at the least? You may enquire there as to the condition of the highways.'

'I shan't go by way of Worcester. I'll cut across the fields, and gain the Pershore road.' Then seeing how crestfallen he looked: 'I ask you not to fret, Childers. I'm not yet in my dotage. The ride will be good for my lungs, and the horse needs the exercise.'

Defeated, he lowered his gaze, just as Hester appeared from the kitchens. My carrying-bag was ready, filled with my necessities: change of clothing, linen and hose, a spare cloak and the volume of Cicero which was my current reading. The stable boy had put up a feed-bag for Leucippus, I was told; there was a flask of watered wine to hang from my saddle, and a leather mug. I nodded, looking at the two of them; I was eager to be gone, and yet felt a pang of regret at leaving. Here, apart from Anne, were the only people I loved.

'It's but a week, or a little more,' I said, forcing a smile. 'That should be enough to conclude whatever business awaits me. As for my daughter's husband, a few days in his company would be more than enough. Now, let's make our farewells.'

Which we did; and a short time later I was in the saddle urging Leucippus to a canter, Thirldon was behind me and a hundred and twenty miles stretched ahead: Pershore, Tetsworth, High Wycombe, Uxbridge, Hillingdon, Brentford, and then Tyburn, with the tower of St Pauls in view.

I confess that a strange hunger was upon me: not merely the desire to see my daughter and her child, but one which I scarce understood. Was it a wish to feel young again, riding into the wind as I had delighted to do as a boy? Or to be in London and hear the roar of Cheapside, walk among fashionable folk at the Exchange, or visit the theatres? Or was it merely the sentiment of an educated man who was beginning to suspect that he has spent too long in the Provinces?

I have said this was my Year of Astonishment, though it began inauspiciously enough. The journey took nearer three days, being slowed by a downpour on the last day, and soured by the poor quality of the inns where I was obliged to stay the night; but let that pass. Wearied as I was, my spirits rose when I walked a tired Leucippus through the suburbs at Holborn, the crowds growing thicker all the while, and made my way down to Fleet Street with its rumbling carts and the shouts of draymen. I turned eastward to ascend Ludgate Hill, arriving at last at the Bel Savage inn where I would bespeak bed, board and stabling. And if the din, smoke and reek from the city seemed even fouler than I remembered, I set that down to the years I had been away. In the stable yard, stiff and sore from my ride, I dismounted and eyed the ostler who came to take my reins.

'Looks like you've come a long way, sir,' he said in phlegmatic fashion.

'Does it?' I said, somewhat irritably. 'You're mighty observant.'

'Court business, is it?'

'Whatever it is, it's no business of yours,' I answered.

'True, master, very true.' He admired Leucippus with a practised eye. 'Shall I give this fine fellow a good rub down after he's had a rest and a drink?'

'You may,' I said.

He waited until I opened my purse and produced a coin, then made his bow and led the horse away. Whereupon, instead of venturing inside the inn, I walked from the yard, under the archway and out into the noise of the street. The light was growing dim, lanterns showed in places, and the curfew would not be long in coming. To stretch my legs, I walked a short distance past the turning to Old Bailey, and stood looking through Ludgate. In truth, all seemed much as it had been when I was last there... so what did I feel, that was different?

Was it my fancy, or was there a rawness and a harshness in the air, along with the smoke and smells of the roaring city – home, it was now said, to two hundred thousand souls? The streets had always been hard; there were beggars at the gate, but there had always been beggars, as there had always been mire and filth, the runnels foul from the day's rain. Then, it was no longer the London I had roamed as a student; a man of my years, who was born in the reign of Queen Mary and grew to manhood under the Glorious Eliza, should not have expected otherwise. This was the London of James, the Sixth of Scotland and the First of England, whom I had never seen; James of the House of Stuart, *Rex Pacificus* as he liked to style himself, ruler by divine right, author of books on tobacco and witches, father of prince and princess and lover, so rumour had it, of handsome young men as well as his Danish queen – and the fount of all wisdom and justice, as he would have his subjects believe. I'll admit that now, I have other names for him.

I turned about and walked back to the inn, my riding boots so muddied that I cared not for splashes made by hoof or foot. I would clean myself, dine and rest, and in the morning I would walk to Shoe Lane, the entrance of which was a mere two hundred yards away, along Fleet Street. There I would enquire after Thomas Jessop, that being his last known address, and see if it bore fruit, though I had small expectation that it would. Hence, I believed, I would have discharged my obligation, though in truth I still failed to see it as such. And I would then be free to ride out to Highgate, to the house of George Bull, husband to my daughter Anne and father of my only grandchild.

Beyond that I had no particular resolve; and yet life is a mingled yarn, as the poet says. Turn it about as I have done, many times since, I could not have foreseen the tangled web that lay ahead of Robert Belstrang, one-time Justice of Worcestershire.

I was about to receive an education, in my sixty-second year, that would alter forever my view of what is fair and good, and what is not.

THREE

The day was one of weak sunlight, after more rain had passed in the night. Having looked in at the stable to see Leucippus was well tended, I made my way down Fleet Street, past St Bride's church as far as the conduit where people gathered. To their eyes, I suspect, I was not a former Justice; merely a gentleman on foot who, despite his good cloak, high-crowned hat and basket-hilt rapier, was without a train or even a servant, and therefore of small consequence. Then, whatever foibles I possess, I like to think vanity is not among them.

From Fleet street I turned into Shoe Lane, the narrow way which led northward to Holborn Hill. The terrain was familiar enough: the Inns of Court, including my own college of Grays Inn, were not far off. People passed by me: huswives with their baskets, prentice boys on errands for their masters. After glancing up the street as far as St Andrews, I stopped at the first house and knocked. It was opened by a harried-looking woman, to whose skirts a brood of children clung. I asked about Thomas Jessop, a lodger hereabouts, but she shrugged; the name meant nothing. I went to the next house, and the next, then crossed the street and repeated my enquiries. The answer was the same: the person was not known here.

Realising that I should offer a description, at the next house I spoke of Jessop as a stocky youth with thick black hair, as was his father's once; I did not mention his Papism. Yet the answers multiplied: nobody could recall anyone of such appearance. Until, that is, I had passed more than half-way up the street, and was growing mighty tired of importuning householders like a common debt-collector. Not only was this beneath me, I thought: it was foolishness. I could almost hear Childers' disapproving voice: *A gentleman does not sully his hands*. I was on the point of giving up the exercise when – as is so often the case - matters changed abruptly.

I had banged on a door, perhaps more violently than was proper, and found myself confronted by an angry-looking man in a dirty apron, an artisan of some kind. Taking in my appearance, he modified his expression and allowed me to state my business, whereupon a reply came readily.

'The glass-painter's house, where the gormand lives. They had a lodger, last year... it might be him.'

'Gormand?' I repeated, in some puzzlement.

'Henry Biershaw's the glass-painter,' my informant said. 'His son is the gormand... you'll know when you see him.' He leaned out of the doorway and pointed up the street, towards Holborn. 'Two – no, three houses from the end.'

Abruptly the door was closed upon me. So, resigned to seeing my enquiry through, I walked up Shoe Lane, counted three houses from its end and rapped upon what I prayed would be the last door. To my disappointment, nobody answered. I knocked again, with similar result, then in frustration I pounded it, disliking the notion that if nobody was home, I should have to return. I was on the point of turning away when the squeal of a latch stayed me, and the door opened to a width of six or seven inches.

'Can I aid you, master?'

The speaker was a scarecrow of a man, peering at me through rheumy eyes; indeed, from the way he squinted, I surmised that he was half-blind. I told my business, for the tenth or eleventh time; by then I had lost count.

'There's no room for a lodger here now, sir,' was his reply. 'I did think you'd come on account of Colley.'

'You had a lodger last year,' I retorted. 'Your neighbours have confirmed it: a young man of stocky build, black-haired. His name is Jessop.'

A pause followed, then: 'I have no acquaintance of that name.'

I looked into the fellow's eyes. After many years at the bench, I pride myself on being able to tell a liar from a truthful man. This one appeared to fall into the latter category, yet one can seldom be certain. I was on the point of forming another question, when something caught my eye. It was nothing more than a glimpse: of a very thin chain of silver, showing at one side of the man's neck inside his shirt collar, but it was enough.

'Perhaps the one who stayed here used a different name,' I said. 'It would not be so unusual for a Catholic, like yourself.'

He blinked, but made no reply.

'See now, Master Biershaw,' I said, in a conciliatory tone. 'I've no business here other than to find the young man I have described. His family are most concerned for him... you might understand, as I hear you have a son yourself. Will you not give me some morsel of news, to take back to them? I've come a very long way.'

More blinking followed, but I saw no guile in this man's expression; rather he seemed to be an open book, one who would be a dismal failure as a gamester. Finally, he opened the door a little wider and spoke.

'We did have a lodger last year, sir, somewhat as you picture him. He left us in the autumn, just before All Souls Day. His name was Philip Mayne. More than that, I cannot tell you.'

'Philip Mayne,' I repeated, frowning.

'That was the name he gave.'

'And how long was he here?'

'Not long, sir... a matter of some weeks.'

'And you haven't seen him since he left?'

'I have not.'

'Then, can you explain how a package of possessions was sent to his family in Worcestershire, containing a letter written from here, signed by Thomas Jessop?'

Henry Biershaw shook his head again - rather quickly, to my mind. 'I cannot, sir. I know of no letter. Nor do I know where Master Mayne might be now...'

But he broke off, flinching at my expression. Falling into old habits, I placed a hand on my sword-hilt and eyed him.

'How would it be if I swore out a warrant for your arrest, for harbouring a Papist fugitive?' I said. 'It strikes me that the evidence is sufficient, since that young man is neither of age, nor had his father's leave to travel. What do you say now?'

Before he could answer there was a commotion from indoors: voices raised, then footsteps. The master of the house turned to speak over his shoulder, but at once the door was wrenched aside, almost throwing him off balance. There stood a stout woman in a workaday frock, her face taut.

'Are you come from the bailiff?' she demanded. 'We've done naught unlawful – I'll swear to it...' She stopped, taking in my appearance as others had: I was no bailiff's man, nor a lackey of any sort. Drawing breath, she moderated her voice.

'Your pardon, master... Is it to do with Colley?'

Despite my indignation, my curiosity was aroused by further mention of that name. Before the woman's husband could speak, I said: 'You're Mistress Biershaw – might I assume that Colley is your son?' Then, recalling the words of the aproned man down the street: 'Is he the gormand?'

'He is, sir,' Mistress Biershaw answered. 'But he don't do his act now, unless for private show.' She glanced at her husband, who had grown agitated.

'It's not on account of Colley,' he said. 'The gentleman's asking after Philip Mayne - sent by his family. I've told him we never saw him after All Souls.'

A silence fell, so that I was aware of the noise of the street, and the clop of hooves from Holborn. Both husband and wife were uneasy now, and I was curious to know why. I decided on a different course, and lifted a conciliatory hand.

'Let me assure you, mistress – and you, Master Biershaw - that I mean you no harm. Might I come inside and speak with you further? If you will tell me what you know, likely I'll not need to trouble you again. Nor...' - this with my most knowing expression – 'does the matter of your religion concern me. If I might recall the words of our late, lamented Queen: I make no windows into men's souls. Do we understand one another?'

'Perhaps we do, sir – after a fashion,' Biershaw replied. And lowering his gaze, he stepped back so that I might enter.

I will speak now of the gormand: Colley Biershaw, a boy of some twenty years. I say *boy* because, despite his great height and girth, the head like a massive pumpkin and hands that could have picked up a man and squeezed the life out of him, this was a child by any other definition: a bloated, red-faced child in a jerkin too small for him, stretched tight across his chest. Barely had I entered the house than a figure loomed up from somewhere and towered above me, so that my instinct was to jerk backwards. Mistress Biershaw, however, hastened to reassure me.

'There's no harm in him, sir, not a jot. He's wary of visitors... I pray you will take his hand, and show him you're a friend.'

I looked up, into a fleshy face with pig-like eyes and a loose mouth. But there was no threat: it was the visage of an innocent - a gargantuan *putto*. Taking a calming breath I put out a hand, half-expecting it to be crushed in a wrestler's hold. But the man-boy took it gently, barely squeezing it before he let go.

'I'm honoured, captain,' were his words.

'He does call most men captain,' Mistress Biershaw said hurriedly. 'Has done ever since he went for a soldier.'

As if to stem his wife's sudden volubility, Henry Biershaw interposed himself, bidding me take a stool at the table. There was some mention of refreshment, but I declined. 'I've no wish to delay you from your work,' I told him. 'I hear you're a painter on glass... I'd not thought there were any left, in these times.'

The Biershaws, husband and wife, sat down at their old table facing me. Their son retreated to a stool in the corner, from where he watched us with interest. Fixing me with a rueful look, my host said: 'I might say that I'm the last glass-painter left about London, sir, yet it would be an untruth. There are others, even if the need for those skilled in decorating church windows is gone. Some rich men will have their arms painted on glass in their great houses, but such work is rare.'

'He does take other tasks – helping the Italians in the city,' Mistress Biershaw broke in, plainly in her husband's defence. 'We're not yet driven to penury.'

But when I turned to look at her, the woman flushed and averted her gaze, and glancing round the bare room, I understood. No doubt the Italian glassmakers, being of the same faith, had been merciful to Biershaw when others were not, but the evidence was plain: this family were as poor as beggars.

'Tell me of your lodger,' I said, to urge matters forward. 'The young man you knew as Philip Mayne. How did he come to stay here?'

'He was directed to my house,' Biershaw said, after some

hesitation. 'We had a room to offer, last year, but the case is altered somewhat...' He hesitated, as there came a stirring from the corner, and Colley the giant spoke up.

'He was my friend, was Philip.'

'Indeed?' I turned, and saw that he was smiling. ''Were you sad at his leaving?'

But in this attempt to engage the youth in conversation, I had erred. There was a sudden tautness from his parents, while Colley's smile faded. 'He was my friend,' he repeated – whereupon to my astonishment he reached down, tore off one of his shoes and began to gnaw at it!

In disbelief I stared, as Mistress Biershaw rose at once and flew at him, struggling to pull the shoe from his hands. His father remained seated, eyes downcast – and I surmised that this behaviour was not unknown, either to man or wife. The tussle in the corner grew more heated, Colley giving vent to muttered protests while his mother remonstrated with him. In the end she was the victor, stepping back with the shoe which she raised aloft. 'You shall have bread soon,' she said breathlessly. 'Now be still, and show respect for our guest.'

I was confounded by the display- until I remembered. 'Your pardon for my haste, Master Biershaw,' I said, after some moments had passed. 'When I heard one speak of your son as a gormand, I thought-'

'That he spoke of mere gluttony,' my host finished, with an edge of bitterness in his voice. 'Would that it were so.'

He paused, then peered at me again with his weak eyes. 'When he went as a soldier, he became notorious. His ensign cast him out, and harshly too, calling him *ganeo mirus* – omnivore, that means. They said Colley did break up his helmet and eat it for a wager – which was small surprise to us. We'd hoped the army would make him change his ways, but it was not to be.'

I began to understand. 'And so, when you said that he no longer does his act...?' I glanced at Mistress Biershaw who, flustered, had retaken her seat.

'He performed at fairs,' Biershaw told me. 'He would eat anything he was given: grass, ashes, twigs, paper and leather –

even to nails and broken glass, live hornets and spiders. But we stopped it.'

'*I* stopped it, sir,' Mistress Biershaw stated. 'Our son was no more than a performing dog to the rabble, who paid their halfpennies to gape and jeer at him. Since then we allow only certain gentlemen to hire him, for private feasts…' she met my eye with a look of defiance.

'He's the Benjamin of our family - born when I was close on forty years, and unfit for more child-bearing. Our older children are grown and gone – yet it was God's will that we should make our home Colley's home for as long as we both live, since he is unfit for any trade. What happens then, is His will also.'

Now that the picture was clear, I had no words; each man and woman has their cross, and this family's was heavy enough. Thereafter I avoided looking at Colley lest I disturb him again. Eager to conclude my business and be gone, I returned to the matter of Thomas Jessop, or Philip Mayne as he was known here, but there appeared to be little more these people could tell me. He had been sent to them, no doubt by another Catholic, as a family of the same faith with whom he might lodge. The letter, if dated correctly as on the Feast of Simon the Apostle, appeared to have been written a mere day or two before he left their house. His stay had been short but pleasant enough, both Biershaws insisted. They liked the young man, who had been good with Colley; he would talk to him, they said. Beyond that, Biershaw repeated, there was nothing of importance to say.

'And you would swear an oath to that?' I asked suddenly, fixing him with a bland look. I had not forgotten my impression, on arrival, that the man knew more than he had revealed. And at mention of the word *oath* I sensed unease again, from both husband and wife.

'I would prefer it if you took what I've said in good faith, sir,' Biershaw answered. But his gaze wavered, and by instinct I pressed forward.

'A solemn oath is what I would prefer,' I told him. 'Perhaps I should have announced myself sooner: my name is Belstrang. I was formerly a Justice of Worcestershire, and I'm a close neighbour of the father of that young man. I'm certain now that he is the one whom you knew as Philip Mayne.'

They were both silent. In the corner I heard Colley shift his great bulk upon the stool, which creaked alarmingly. Without taking my eyes off Biershaw, I demanded that if he knew anything further about his former lodger, particularly his likely whereabouts, he should tell me now or face the consequences. There followed a moment, then answer came – not from him, but from his guileless son.

'You'd best seek out Mistress Jane – for he did love her!'

I looked, and saw the man-boy nodding at me. 'He did love her,' he repeated. 'Kind Mistress Jane...' he frowned, and looked to his father.

'When will she come again?' he asked. 'Why does she not come?'

Biershaw did not answer him, but threw a look at his wife, who gave a great sigh of weariness. 'We should tell the gentleman,' she said finally. 'Likely he'll find out soon enough, by the look of him.' And when I raised my eyebrows at her, she said:

'There is a widow in Holborn named Jane Rudlin. It was she who sent Philip to us, after being asked if she knew of lodging for one newly come to London.'

I shifted my gaze to Henry Biershaw, who looked so forlorn I had to pity him. The man was torn between telling the truth and protecting one of his faith, and with good reason: had I been of a vindictive disposition, I might have made difficulties for him. I pondered a little, then:

'Is what Colley says true? Was Philip Mayne this woman's lover?'

'No, sir, he was not.' On that point Biershaw was firm. 'Mistress Rudlin is a good soul, who cares only for her young daughter. She was a friend to Philip, and he would visit her at times - there was nothing untoward.'

'Could it be that when he left your house last year, it was to her that he went?'

'In God's name, Master Belstrang, I do not know,' Biershaw replied. 'But I will tell you-'

He stopped abruptly: his wife had placed a hand upon his arm.

Blinking, he half-turned to her, whereupon she faced me and spoke up.

'I fear we must make request of you, sir. My husband is an honest man, who sometimes speaks too readily. Yet it would soothe my mind if you would promise not to involve us further in the matter of Philip Mayne, whatever your purpose. We would of course take your word, as a gentleman. We are poor folk, and easy prey... but you know that well enough.'

A moment passed, while they both waited. In the corner, seemingly intrigued by the close talk at the table, Colley was silent. Whereupon, somewhat in spite of my better judgement, I nodded and gave them assurance.

'Whatever I learn, none shall know from whose lips it came,' I stated. 'My desire is but to get word of an impetuous young man, whether he be alive or dead, and carry the news to his father and mother. Like you, they are devoted to their son, and distraught at having no word of him.'

'Well and good, sir...' In some relief, Biershaw nodded in turn. 'Then I will say this: when Philip left here, he told us he would not return – that he had a purpose in mind, of which he could not speak. Nor would he say where he was bound; and moreover, he said that if we did chance to see him again, we would not know him – those were his words. At the last he asked us to pray for him, and urged us to be of good cheer, for there was much to hope for. That's the nub of it, and it was indeed a sad farewell, for Colley most of all. Now I've told everything... have I not?'

The question was addressed to his wife, who barely nodded. Whereupon the two of them sat and regarded me, as if to show that their consciences were clear, and I could expect nothing more.

'Very well.' I rose from the table, and gave them thanks for aiding me. 'But you understand that when I go to Mistress Rudlin, as I soon will, she will likely know who directed me to her.'

That fact, however, seemed not to trouble my hosts, who no doubt relied on the discretion of a fellow Papist, as I surmised this woman must be. They too stood up, not troubling to hide their relief. I would find Jane Rudlin near Furnival's Inn, I was told: a very small house, just inside the turning to Portpoole. They meant the narrow lane to Grays Inn, which I knew well.

On the doorstep, another thought occurred to me. 'Did Philip pay for his bed and board promptly?' I asked Biershaw. 'Or was he tardy?'

'He was never tardy,' the man answered. 'He was a generous youth... always willing to open his purse.'

He was about to go inside when Colley lumbered up to the doorway, still wearing only one shoe. Almost pushing his father aside he extended his hand, like a great slab of raw beef. 'Goodbye, captain,' he said as I took it. 'My friend.'

Giving them both farewell, I walked quickly off down Shoe Lane; only then did the aptness of that name strike home. I might have laughed, had the heavens not opened almost at once, and wet my face with raindrops. My mind busy, I was at the junction with Fleet Street again before I realized I was going in the wrong direction. I had recalled John Jessop's testimony: that his son was all but penniless when he left home. So - whence came this money, with which he was reported to be generous?

I was caught in the shower, great splashes of rain drumming on my hat, but I barely noticed it; I knew now that I was on a quest, and driven by more than a desire to bring some comfort to a distraught neighbour. My curiosity was aroused, and I wished to sate it.

My visit to Mistress Rudlin should wait until the afternoon, I decided, and be undertaken on a full stomach.

FOUR

The house was indeed small, and quite humble. The rain-shower had passed as I sat in the warmth of an inn on the Strand, where I took dinner. Thus fortified, I walked by way of Fetter Lane up to Holborn and turned into Portpoole: a place of crowded tenements where many of the poorer countrymen of King James have long settled, hence its nickname of Little Scotland. Thinking that this was an odd place for a Papist like Mistress Rudlin to dwell, I halted and rapped on the door, which was answered promptly enough.

The woman who faced me was perhaps forty years old, tall and dignified. Her plain black gown rose to the neck, which was unadorned. She showed no surprise at seeing a man of my station on her doorstep, and in a somewhat dour manner affirmed that she was the person I sought. On hearing that I was come from Henry Biershaw, the glass-painter, her expression did not alter. But when I named the youth who went by the name of Philip Mayne, she tensed.

'I've not seen him for many months, sir.'

'Yet you and he were friends, I understand.'

'And if we were, what of it?'

Somewhat impatiently, I told her my station and spoke of my search. 'His father had a letter from him, written at the Biershaw house at the end of October last, but received only days ago. It was included in a package of belongings... do you know anything of that?'

To my displeasure she gave no answer but merely stood her ground, and I found it hard to read her expression. 'If you do, you would be well advised to tell me,' I persisted. 'The young man's father and mother are driven close to distraction by their son's disappearance – they even fear he may be dead. For charity's sake, if nothing more, will you speak of-'

'He is not dead.'

The words were out quickly, and to my eyes the woman appeared to regret uttering them. She was about to add something, then seemed to think better of it. Seizing the moment, putting aside the great relief I felt, I leaned towards her.

'Then where is he?' I demanded. 'If you know, you must tell me.'

She took a breath. 'And if I will not?'

'Then I will take steps to have you questioned.'

'Steps?' Her eyebrows lifted a little. 'Do you threaten me, sir?'

'You may be certain of it,' I answered. 'If you refuse to tell me his whereabouts, you flout the law. As a former Justice, I can carry the matter forward-'

With some weariness, the woman relented. 'Very well - I will tell you what I can, but the news is not pretty,' she said. 'Nor will it offer any comfort to Thomas's family.' And when I showed my surprise:

'Yes, I know his true name is Thomas Jessop. As for what else I might know, sir, it matters little, for your quest is fruitless. I would urge you to return to his father, and tell him...' She hesitated, then:

'Tell him a lie. Tell him his son is dead – that would be best for everyone. For he is lost to this world already - and if God is merciful, he will likely die soon in any case.'

I was confounded; her words, despite making little sense, were as doom-laden as any I'd heard. And more, I was growing angry with the woman's manner.

'You dare ask such of me?' I returned. 'I will lie to no-one, especially a neighbour and a-' I checked myself, surprised at the way my mind ran - 'and a friend,' I finished. 'And most particularly in a matter of such gravity. Besides, were his son dead, Jessop would wish me to bring his body home. You speak in riddles... tell me where to find Thomas, and waste no more of my time.'

I waited; Mistress Rudlin, for her part, refused to meet my gaze. I saw her hand stray by instinct to her neck, before she collected herself.

'He is confined,' she said at last. 'In the hospital of St Mary of Bethlehem.'

'In Bedlam?' I stared at her, my thoughts whirling. 'How can that be? By whose order was he confined? Tell me!'

At that, her mouth hardened. 'If you mean by whose lawful direction, it was by the constables who took him off to Bridewell, and those who sent him thence to Bedlam. But if you mean otherwise, I might say that he confined himself. For he was lost... he's a soul unmoored, who must be brought back to his maker.'

She lifted her gaze, then: 'No doubt you'll wish to go the hospital and discover the matter for yourself. But I will say that there's nothing you can do for Thomas except pray for him, sir, as do I – every day. Now please, leave me.'

Lost for words, with the news still settling in my mind, I made no answer. Nor did I attempt to stay her when she bobbed her head, stepped back and was about to close the door upon me. Then she paused, and said:

'If you do venture there, it's best to go in the morning... there will be visitors at this hour, and the noise is fearful. The porters will be too overtaxed to aid you... accost them in the morning, early.'

And she was gone.

That evening, after taking a supper, I sat in my room at the Bel Savage and tried to gather my thoughts, aided by a jug of wine. Below me the inn roared: someone was playing a lute, the company providing a chorus. Having bespoken pen, ink and paper, I sat at a small table and thought to compose a letter to John Jessop, but soon abandoned the notion: I would wait until I had seen his son for myself and confirmed Jane Rudlin's testimony, grim as it was.

For the very thought of Bedlam chilled me, and it does still: a place of torment where the distracted are kept until they either come to their senses, or are removed by their relatives, or die. Even in my student days I refrained from going to view the inmates, as others did: I had no stomach for such a wretched spectacle; for watching whippings and beatings dealt to those who had committed no crime, except it be in their minds. The knowledge that I had small choice but to go there on the morrow filled me with foreboding – not least for the condition in which I might find Thomas Jessop. I consoled myself with the thought that he was at least alive; and that if I might have him freed by some means, he could be sent to his family where, God willing, in time he might be brought back to himself.

Yet the time-span troubled me. I had neglected to ask Jane Rudlin when Thomas was taken into confinement. Were it as far back as last All Souls, more than four months had passed; and four months spent in Bedlam was something I cared not to think upon. I should have pressed her further, I decided, for it was plain she knew more than she told. Hence, I would approach her again and be firmer in my questioning. But it had to wait – as my visit to Anne at Highgate must now wait.

Still troubled, I put aside pen and paper and retired to my bed, where I was obliged to dull the noise of the inn with more wine before I could sleep. So it was that, somewhat irritable and with a powerful thirst, I rose in the morning and faced the day with foreboding.

Had I truly known what was ahead of me, I think now, I might have put off the whole business and stayed in bed.

The day was cloudy, with a light breeze blowing from the river. I rode to Bedlam, having no desire to muddy my boots again. Leucippus picked his way through the crowded streets; being unused to the noise and press of London, he was as taut as was his master. From the inn we went by Old Bailey to Newgate, and thence passed through the city, along the length of Cheap and Poultry into Three Needle Street. At last, emerging from Bishopsgate, we reached the corner of Houndsditch, with the Dolphin Inn to our right. Ahead was the Hospital: a squat, two-storied building, as devoid of features as it was devoid of promise.

At the doors I dismounted, hearing muffled sounds from within, and called out for the gatekeeper. One came presently: a heavy-bearded, thick-browed man with more of the look of a turnkey than anything else; then, that was small surprise. But when I asked to speak to the Keeper of Bedlam, he shook his head.

'Master Jenner is seldom here, sir. There are but the porters and gallery-maids, along with our charges. May I ask your business? It's too early for visitors.'

'Master Jenner,' I repeated.

'If you wish to leave a message for him, I could have it conveyed,' I was told. 'Three pennies will serve.'

'Well, in truth it's one of your charges I want to see - and in private,' I said, putting a hand on my purse. 'Will three pennies serve for that?'

'It might, master,' the man allowed, without expression. 'Yet much depends on who it is you would see. Some of our charges are ill-disposed towards visitors… are you a relative?'

'A friend come on behalf of his family, that of a young man called-' I checked myself. 'He's Philip Mayne. He was sent from Bridewell.'

At mention of the name, the porter relaxed. 'That can be arranged with ease,' he said. 'More, it will spare you the tedium of passing through the house.'

He pointed to his right, to a small wicket-gate beside the hospital. 'You'll find the churchyard at the end of that lane. Master Philip sits there often, even in the cold. He's given leave, for he has no will to escape.'

To my relief, the business was conducted promptly and without difficulty. The porter, who gave his name as Scantbury, disappeared indoors while I passed through the gate, down a muddy lane and through another gate into the Bedlam Churchyard, last resting place for so many of its inmates. It was a peaceful enough plot, bordered by high walls, and a deep ditch at the rear where it overlooked the open space of Moorfields. It was also deserted, and the single bench by the rear of the main house was unoccupied. Then a door opened and Scantbury appeared, leading a slight, shambling figure by the arm - one I did not recognise at all until the two of them drew close, whereupon I gave a start.

'Thomas?' I exclaimed. 'Is it you?' Then, remembering, I faced the porter in some haste. 'It's a nickname… I thought he would respond to it.'

But the man merely shrugged. 'It's of no import, sir, for he never listens, nor does he speak to anyone. You might address him as Lord Treasurer for all the difference it makes.' Turning to his charge, he said: 'Sit down, Philip, and let this gentleman sit beside you. He wishes only to talk.'

He led Thomas Jessop – for it was he, I realised, despite the changes I saw in him – to the bench and let go of his arm. Whereupon the youth sat, staring at nothing. In consternation I addressed Scantbury again.

'How long-' I began, but quickly he forestalled me.

'He came to us about Michaelmas. They could do naught with him – the beadles of Bridewell, that is. He would tell them nothing - though they knew his name, I know not how. He never made a sound, even when beaten, nor has he since coming here. He won't even eat now. They say someone tried to poison him at Bridewell… another prisoner stole his food, and was mighty sick from it.'

In dismay I looked upon the still and silent figure of Thomas Jessop, whom it seemed I must continue to call Philip Mayne, and felt my spirits sink. Jane Rudlin's words flew to my mind: *he is lost to this world already, and will likely die soon…*

'He won't eat, you say?' I found myself frowning. 'Then, what steps do you take? Is he to be allowed to die of hunger, or…?'

'What would you have us do?' Scantbury countered. 'Stuff bread down his gullet till he chokes?' He glanced at his charge, who gave no sign of hearing. 'He drinks water when it's near, otherwise he seems to want nothing. He used to pray when he was first here: at night, when he thought no one saw him, I was told. Now he does little but sit and sleep… he barely shits.' He paused, then: 'Could be he was praying to St Joseph for a good death.'

For a moment I did not understand the man's meaning; then as the words sank home I opened my mouth, but again he forestalled me.

'I've seen it before, master, and no doubt I'll see it again: the boy wants to die. Others have taken their lives in here… but he's a devout fellow, isn't he? Or was once, they say. He knows it's a mortal sin so he's put himself in the Lord's hands, and awaits His mercy.'

'Mercy?' With some bitterness I mouthed the word, half to myself. 'It appears to me he's been shown precious little of that.' Looking Scantbury in the eye, I said: 'He was beaten at Bridewell, you say – is he beaten here, too?'

'Seldom, nowadays,' came the vague reply; the man was as free of shame as he was of pity. 'Not as others are, for it did no good. I told you: he makes no sound, whatever befalls him.' Then, clearly thinking he had more than earned his three pennies, he turned to go.

'I will be inside, close to that door, should you need me,' he said, with a jerk of his head towards the building. 'I'll wait a quarter of an hour before I return, though I wager you'll not need so long as that.'

I waited until he had gone indoors before sitting down, I confess nervously. The bench was half-rotten and sagged with my weight, but there was no stir from Thomas Jessop. His gaze appeared to be fixed on the horizon, or at least as far as Moorfields where, at this hour, men exercised their dogs. Since he appeared not to notice my presence I took time to survey him, and was sobered by what I saw.

For this was not the youth I had known, back in Worcestershire; a boy of vigour, who liked to swim in the river and walk in the Malvern Hills, known even from a distance by his mane of thick, crow-black hair. To begin with, his hair had been shaved, leaving a dirty stubble scarred with old cuts, I guessed from a blunt razor. If his beard too had been shorn it had barely sprouted since, being but a youthful and wispy growth. He indeed looked half-starved, his face as thin as his frame, the arms like wands in his loose sleeves. As for his clothing: I was unsurprised by its filthiness or its stink: what surprised me was the fact that he seemed utterly untroubled by either. It occurred to me then that this might be some form of penance he was undergoing.

Gazing at him, in pity and with growing helplessness, I thought on his father, and the speech we'd had back at Thirldon almost a week ago. Thomas Jessop, the scion of Papists, was indeed a devout fellow as Scantbury had said: fierce in his faith, filled with admiration for martyrs like Oldcorne, whose execution he had witnessed. What was it, I wondered, that had brought him to London to dwell among strangers - let alone to end up in such a wretched case? And if he would not speak, even to one he knew from his home county, what then should I do?

I resolved that I would try, at least.

'Thomas,' I said, speaking close. 'It's Justice Belstrang... I'm come from your father. Do you not know me?'

There was no response; not even the flicker of an eyelid.

'They are beside themselves with fretting after you – your father and your mother,' I said. 'Have you no message for them? Is there no word that I can take back to Worcester?'

My answer – or the lack of it - was the same.

'If you can hear me, I pray you will me give me a sign,' I persisted, lifting my voice. 'Do you mean to stay here until you die? Is that truly your desire?'

There came a sigh, and nothing more. The air was damp and somewhat chill, yet he barely shivered. It was as if he were present in body, yet his mind was shut away elsewhere. With a growing sense of despair, I tried again.

'You should know that Jane Rudlin told me of your whereabouts. I spoke with her, as I did with Henry Biershaw and his wife, with whom you lodged. They wish for your recovery... especially Colley. He was your friend, was he not?'

At that my hopes stirred: was there a flicker of recognition? Unconsciously I leaned further forward, then drew back in dismay. For his response, unwitting or not, was eloquent enough: tears welled from his eyes, and spilled over on to his pale cheeks. He uttered no sound, but the picture was one I would remember for the rest of my days: Thomas was in torment, and a prisoner of it. *Why this is hell,* said Mephistopheles in the play of Faustus; *nor am I out of it.*

'Forgive me,' I said at last, and stood up. And though the poor Bedlamite gave no sign of caring whether I stayed or went, I asked him if I might return.

'Is there aught you need?' I said, looking down upon him.

'Anything at all?'

I waited, without much hope of an answer – and at last gained my reward, though it was nothing more than a slow turn of the head in my direction. Yet no words followed, nor did Thomas's eyes seek mine; his gaze remained dull and empty.

And so I left him and moved towards the rear of the hospital, thinking what further questions I might put to Scantbury. Barely had I drawn near the door, however, than it opened and the man appeared, before the agreed time was up. It being plain to him what had occurred, he merely nodded and began to move towards the bench, but I stayed him.

'His bed and board,' I said. 'Who pays for it, the parish?'

He gave one of his shrugs. 'I know naught of it, save that his charge is three shillings a week. You'd need to ask Master Jenner whence it comes.'

'I will,' I told him. 'As I will inform Philip's father of his condition – I might say his plight.' My anger was growing somewhat. 'Since he doesn't eat, you say, I wonder how the three shillings is spent. Does no-one even trouble to wash him?'

But Scantbury was indifferent to my sensibilities. 'It's not my place,' he said. 'Now, if your business is done here, I'll take him inside.'

'And more,' I said, raising a hand, 'I will set in motion the means for his release into my custody. If I had my way now, he'd not spend another day in this place.'

'As you please, master,' the other replied, in an easy tone. 'Yet, being as you're not a relative, you would need a signed order to take him, issued by the rightful persons.'

'Then I will get it,' I said.

At the entry to the lane I stopped and turned, to watch Scantbury lead his charge back inside. He went willingly enough, but at the entrance he paused and looked in my direction, whereupon the porter gave him a shove through the open doorway. From within came a chorus of shouting, fit for a host of demons. Sick at heart, I walked the lane back to Bishopsgate Street, and to the comforting presence of Leucippus.

In truth, I was in a quandary how to break the news to John

Jessop. I had no doubt that, whatever case his son was in, he would want him brought home. I would write to him at once, but his written order to have Thomas pass into my keeping would take time to come – perhaps a week or more. In the meantime, what was I to do?

For there was a puzzle here; something that did not sit right. For one thing, who was it paid for Thomas's keep - and why would they do so? Moreover, I was as yet unclear why he was taken prisoner in the first place, to be incarcerated in Bridewell – by the constables, Jane Rudlin had said. How did she know he had since been sent to Bedlam, unless she had visited him?

I would return to her, and find out. And once again, my visit to my daughter would have to wait.

FIVE

When Mistress Rudlin found me on her doorstep again that afternoon her displeasure was evident, but I was in no humour for evasion. Having given her a concise account of my visit to Bedlam, I demanded she tell me everything she knew of Thomas Jessop, or I would return with a warrant for her arrest. And though my legal grounds for such might have been tenuous, the bluff was effective enough.

'Must it be now?' she said, lowering her gaze. 'I have company…'

She broke off, and I grew aware of voices inside the house. Seeing my questioning look, she said: 'I teach children their letters. If you would care to return later…'

'I would not,' I said. Then as her words sank home: 'Do you mean you tutor the children of Papists? For that alone may be a matter worthy of investigation.'

'Their letters, and simple mathematics – nothing more,' Mistress Rudlin insisted, her mouth tightening. But seeing I was not to be gainsaid, she gave a sigh. 'Then, I see you must have your way. Will you wait while I dismiss them?'

I stood in the street, as people went by and dogs scratched in the dirt. Soon there came a tide of chatter along with the rattle of footsteps, and four or five boys emerged from the house, looking curiously at me as they passed. When the last had gone the mistress herself appeared, and allowed me to enter. I did so, finding myself in a very small room with only a table, stools and a chest. Seated at the table was a girl of perhaps twelve or thirteen years, eying me warily.

'She is my daughter,' Mistress Rudlin said. Turning to the child, she bade her take her hornbook upstairs so that she could have private discourse with the visitor. Without a word the girl went out, whereupon her mother faced me, folding her hands before her in prim composure. Not being invited to sit, I stood facing her.

'You too have seen Thomas, in that vile place,' I ventured.

And when the woman made no reply: 'How did you know he was sent there from Bridewell?'

'Gossip...' she gave a shake of her head. 'I forget who told me – does it matter?'

'What was he to you?' I asked her. 'The boy, Colley Biershaw... he said Thomas loved you. Were you merely his friend, or were you his lover?'

'I was not, sir.' Jane Rudlin answered, most firmly 'And if you think so badly of me, I wonder that you believe anything I tell you.'

'Indulge me,' I said. 'First, I'll ask how he came to you, last year. He had never been in London before, and to his father's knowledge he knew no-one here. What do you say to that?'

'That he was a young man in need of a place to sleep, who was travel-weary and afraid,' she said. 'It was no more than a Christian duty to offer him help.'

'Afraid?' I frowned at her. 'Of what?'

'I do not know, nor did I ask,' was the reply. 'I knew only that Henry Biershaw took lodgers, so I sent him there.'

'Yet they – and everyone else here, I find - knew him by the name he gave: Philip Mayne. You alone seem to know his true name... how is that?'

She hesitated, and I knew she was concealing something. Whereupon, on a whim, I sought to unnerve her. 'The packet, that came to his father by carrier,' I said. 'Was it you who sent it?' And when she failed to answer: 'It contained Popish trappings, among them a crucifix and a rosary. If I had this house searched, would I find similar materials? Might I even find forbidden books?'

She was caught, and she saw that I knew it. A look of weariness passed across her features, which I will confess were attractive enough, even to a man of my years. Her condition, like that of the Biershaws – like that of most people of her faith – was precarious; and yet the woman did not lack courage. Meeting my gaze, she said: 'Search if you will, sir. You'll find naught but a bible, and a volume of Our Lady's Mattins – and yes, a rosary. Are you satisfied?'

'Not yet,' I said. But having profited from this sally, I

moderated my tone. 'Let me say this: I've no desire for any search, nor to bring trouble upon you. My concern is Thomas Jessop, who languishes in a place worse than a gaol, to my mind; in gaol he might at least beg for alms at the gates. And though I've but slight acquaintance with you, I do not believe you want him to remain there, either.'

She was silent at that, which I took for assent. Thus encouraged, I said: 'Will you not help me, so that I might help Thomas? His family are ill with worry – and I don't concur with the notion that it would be better if they believed him dead. Moreover, I have seen Bedlam Churchyard - and I do not believe it a fitting place for his burial.'

'No… it is not,' Jane Rudlin admitted. And as I watched, she took a step back and sank down on a stool.

'I sent the package to Master Jessop,' she said, speaking low. 'I placed the letter inside because I believed it was the last letter Thomas would write, and that his father should have it.'

I gazed at her, until she looked away. 'Do you tell me that you were the last person to see him, before he was made a prisoner?' I demanded.

'It may be so,' she answered.

'And, he left the letter in your keeping?'

She nodded.

'Then why did you wait?' I went on, turning the matter about as I spoke. 'Why leave it so long-'

'Because I went to see him in the hospital, as you surmise,' she broke in. 'Three times I went – the last time little more than a fortnight ago, after which I lost all hope of his recovering his senses. He appeared to have no desire to leave there, ever.' And her expression changed – to my eyes, into one of anguish.

'His mind is enmeshed in a web of his own making. I told you: he is lost, and only God's mercy can save him.'

'Did you read the letter?' I asked, after a moment's thought.

'Well now, how should I answer that?' She countered. 'If I deny it, you will think I lie. Whereas if I admit it, no doubt I lay myself open to further charges – for you seem convinced I have sinned in some way. Do I hit the mark?'

'I don't speak of sin,' I answered. 'I seek only facts - to whit, who pays for Thomas's board at Bedlam? He's not of this parish, nor any in London. Who would meet the charges, and why?'

'Of that I have no knowledge,' Mistress Rudlin replied. 'And I will swear to it.'

'Very well.' I weighed the matter. 'I still have no inkling as to why he was taken by the constables in the first place. Have you any knowledge of that?'

'I have, but I doubt you would want to convey it to Thomas's father.' She took a breath, and met my eye. 'He was drinking a good deal, by the end of October. I saw more of him in those days, and was concerned for him. He planned to leave the Biershaws, he said, in the first week of November. He was troubled, but would not say why; something pressed upon him, harder as each day passed – until at last it broke him.'

'Broke him – how?'

She shook her head. 'All I can say is that one day he was himself, and the next he was not. Raving, shouting in the street... folk fled from him, fearing he was possessed. The constables came, and smelled the drink on his breath. It might have ended there, with them telling him to go home and sleep it off – until he attacked them.'

She looked away. 'I too feared he was possessed, for this was not the young man I knew. He was like a demon, raging and spouting nonsense.'

'What sort of nonsense?' I demanded.

'A jumble, fit for Babel. One thing I heard distinctly: he cursed himself for a gull, and a dupe. He was still shouting as they bore him away. Only from what I hear, by the time he was inside Bridewell he had lapsed into silence. He's been silent ever since - as you yourself saw.'

I was abashed; the woman's testimony merely served to raise further questions. What, in heaven's name, was I to make of the matter? Though on one point, at least, I was relieved: I'd come to believe she was a truthful woman. Whereupon...

'Did Thomas have a confessor?' I asked. And when my answer was merely a stony expression, I repeated it.

'Come, you make confession yourself when you can, as do all

those of your religion. Did Thomas ever ask you to direct him to a priest?'

'I think you should know better than to ask that of me, sir,' Mistress Rudlin said. 'As you know that if Thomas did make confession, it would be a matter of sanctity, of which his confessor may not speak.'

'Of course I do,' I said, somewhat impatiently. 'As I know there's likely a priest in hiding, a stone's throw from here. But I am no pursuivant - I wish only to know what changed a devout youth into a demon, as you describe him. It could be that by knowing what drove him to such despair, I might be able to help him.'

'I fear only God can help him,' the woman answered. 'I know that I cannot - nor can I aid you further.' She frowned. 'So, will you threaten me now? Even if I did know of a priest, do you think I would tell you willingly?'

I gave no answer; a feeling of disappointment was upon me. Whatever sensibilities I might have harboured in my younger days, I had no stomach for persecuting Papists, let alone for seeing this woman put to hard question. The trail, I sensed, was growing cold, with no further ways open to me. Sifting through what she had said, only a lame question came to mind.

'Is there no-one else who might tell me of Thomas's affairs here? You say he was drinking - was there anyone he befriended?'

'There's one man you might speak with,' Mistress Rudlin answered, after a moment. 'He keeps the fencing hall in Aldersgate Street, where Thomas used to go at times. His name is Richard Elms.'

She stood up, giving me to understand that she would say nothing more. I thanked her; I even asked pardon for disrupting her teaching, and received a courteous reply. Having no desire to stay longer I went to the door, where I stopped.

'You did not tell me whether or not you read Thomas's letter to his father,' I said. And when she did not reply: 'I believe you did, and hence you'll have read of the blow he intended to strike – something that would make his father proud, were his words. Have you any notion of what he meant by that?'

'I have not, sir,' Mistress Rudlin answered.

It was little enough, but for the present it would have to serve.

That night I wrote my letter to John Jessop, sparing few details. If he wished to have his son brought home, I told him, and would give me leave to have Thomas placed in my charge, then I would undertake the business speedily. I could be found at the Bel Savage Inn, where I would await his answer before proceeding. Meanwhile, I added, I might seek the whereabouts of Jenner, the Keeper of Bedlam, for whom I had questions. I was of a mind to assure him that Thomas was in fair health and well cared-for – but that being a lie, I could not bring myself to write it. Having finished the letter and sealed it I paid a servant to deliver it, for fast despatch by post horse. Upon which, mighty weary of the day's exertions, I retired to bed, cheered only by the thought that in the morning I would ride out to Highgate, and at last see my daughter.

And when I did so, for some hours the business of the Jessops fell away, and I tasted joy for the first time since leaving Worcestershire.

Anne was little changed; more precisely, she was less changed than I feared, after the loss of her second child: a son who, had he lived, would have been almost two years old. Her face was a little taut, perhaps, though her smile was as warm as I could have wished. She dressed more soberly now, I noticed, as befitting the wife of a tight-buttoned lawyer like George Bull.

'You're much greyer,' she said, as we embraced. 'Then, so is George – grey beyond his age. A crabbed old Precisian, at less than forty years. I call him that when I'm displeased with him.'

Somewhat surprised, I asked after her husband's health, and was assured that he was well. He was at Westminster Hall, as I had expected; I do not say *hoped*. Seeing that Anne and I would have the day to ourselves, my spirits rose even further.

'And where's my grand-daughter?' I asked. 'Not still abed?'

She was brought at once: a miniature of her mother, down to the cut of her hair, though her attire was less restrained. The servant, a woman in sombre dress, led her into the room by the hand, telling her to remember how to greet a gentleman. Whereupon she was taken aback when I bent down to my pretty Kate, and held out my hands toward her.

'What vision of delight is this?' I exclaimed. 'I'm your grandsire, come more than a hundred miles to see you. Have you no greeting for me?'

For a moment I believed the child would shrink from me – until to my joy she broke into a smile and bobbed a curtsey. 'I'm glad to see you, sir… are you very old?'

The servant drew a sharp breath - but I laughed, as readily as I'd done in years. Whereupon Anne laughed too, while Kate merely looked surprised. And thereafter my joy was complete, as I embraced my daughter's daughter.

We did not speak of the child Anne had lost; or not until later, when we'd taken dinner and were at table together. We had done with exchanging news, such as it was; little happened at Thirldon. Here in Highgate, above the smoke and smells of London, where men of substance had been building fair houses for years, life was pleasant. George, it seemed, had prospered well enough, despite being somewhat out of step with the prevailing tide; an austere man, he had no liking for the Court, nor for the antics of favourites and flatterers. In that respect, if no other, he and I were of similar mind; though in truth I never understood my daughter's attraction for the man. After speaking of George for a time, however, I felt it was time to broach the other matter, and asked Anne how she had fared since her sickness.

'I took a long time to recover,' she said. 'But I was well cared for by Alice – Kate's nurse, whom you have seen. She's a plague widow, who once lost a child herself.' Then, as I was on the point of framing the question that had been on my mind all along, she divined my thoughts.

'I might have come home to Thirldon for a time, as you wished - I have your letter still. I wanted to, but there was much to do once I was well enough to undertake my duties. Kate was growing quickly…'

She broke off; she and I had never deceived each other. For

the truth was plain: it was George who had refused her permission to travel to Worcestershire.

'I understand,' I said, without attempting to hide my feelings. 'You are a dutiful wife, and you do your husband great credit.'

'You'll stay to supper, of course?' Anne asked then, and not merely to change the subject of our discourse. It was her heartfelt wish, I knew, that George and I might strive to get along better; though that, I felt, would involve considerable effort on the part of us both. In short, the man thought me a backwoods Justice who had failed to make the best of an Inns of Court education. More, to a man of his persuasion, I was irreligious; while I thought him a humourless pedant, with a face to match his well-starched ruff. And yet:

'Gladly,' I said. 'No doubt George and I will have much to talk of.'

'Good.' She brightened: 'And how is Hester? You've barely spoken of her.'

'She's well...' I found a smile forming. 'It was she who persuaded me to travel to London.'

'Indeed?' Anne smiled in turn. 'And as always, you could not gainsay her. When I was very small, I once called her a harpy. It was only as I grew older that I saw how much Mother relied on her, and how loyal she was.'

I nodded, not needing to say more.

'But what other business do you have in London? You have been here some days, and only now do you visit us.'

I thought for a moment, before deciding to tell her of my errand on behalf of John Jessop. I said little about what had occurred since my arrival: only that the man's son was in poor health, and that I was intent on sending him home. For her part, Anne was greatly surprised.

'Thomas Jessop? That angry boy, who always got into fights? What does he do in London?'

'I do not know why he came,' I said. 'But it scarcely matters now; all I want is to send him to his father, and be done with it.' Though I knew I was being less than forthright: in truth, the mystery surrounding the wretched Thomas had taken such root in my mind, that I was somewhat keen to get to the nub of it.

Whereupon another notion occurred – but this time Anne's thoughts leaped ahead of mine.

'It's best not to speak of this with George,' she said quietly. 'He would find it hard to understand why you involve yourself in-'

'With Papists,' I finished, to which she had no need to reply. 'You may rest assured, I will not broach it.'

Whereupon with relief she turned to lighter matters. 'Will you seek out other acquaintances while you're here? What of your old friend Master Druett? George sees him sometimes, in the course of legal business. He lives in Coleman Street now, I believe, close to the Armourers' Hall.'

'John Druett? I've not seen him in so long, I doubt he'd remember me.'

'Nonsense,' Anne said. 'You were close – you were at his wedding.'

'Back in 1588,' I replied, surprised myself by the time that had passed. 'Armada Year, when the country went mad - and you were barely a year old.'

'Well, what of it? Such friendships do not fade, only ripen with the years.'

'Or rot,' I said; whereupon on hearing my own words, I let out a snort of laughter. 'Listen to me – I'm but a sour old crab myself.'

'That is so,' Anne said, and rose from her chair; but she was smiling. 'To remedy which, you'd best seek Kate's company, while I give instruction for our supper.'

Thereafter I passed a most pleasant afternoon, until evening fell and George Bull returned home. And since I had not relished the reunion, I would in time be mightily surprised when matters fell the way they did.

Then I speak still of the Year of Astonishment, which had barely begun.

SIX

To say that George looked older, as Anne had said, would fall short; in the years since I'd last seen him, he had aged considerably. The face was fleshier, and he had grown thicker about the waist, as do so many of his profession who spend long hours seated upon their rumps. Yet his greeting was cordial, and supper passed easily enough as we talked of family and of everyday matters. At the end of the meal, with candles lit, and having imbibed freely of George's claret, we fell at last to matters of State, upon which I soon discerned I was too far behind with the news for my son-in-law's liking.

'Surely you have heard that Sir Walter Raleigh has been released from The Tower?' He enquired, raising his brows at me. 'London is talking of little else.'

I had not, I admitted, and though the news was only of passing interest, I invited him to say more.

'After almost thirteen years of incarceration,' George went on. 'Soon after the King came to his throne, and was eager to see the man put away. Not that I hold that godless adventurer in any regard, you understand, but little was ever proven against him. Whereas now...' something close to a sneer appeared. 'Now, on a sudden our King is eager to set him free. The fact that Raleigh offers to go on another voyage to the Americas in pursuit of gold, of course, is mere coincidence.'

'Well, even in far-off Worcestershire we hear talk of the parlous state of the royal coffers,' I said. 'Does the King spend as lavishly as ever?'

Anne, who had been quiet for some time, chose the moment to speak. 'You might indeed say lavishly. The crown is said to be in debt by seven hundred thousand pounds.' She looked to George. 'Is that not so?'

'At the least,' George answered. 'Much of it spent on hunting trips and fripperies, and gifts for favourites – those perfumed popinjays that buzz about Whitehall like blowflies.'

I enjoyed his alliteration, but feared he was getting into his stride; and soon enough, he began to talk of recent scandals. Like most people I had heard of the fall from grace of the King's favourite the Earl of Somerset, as I knew that Villiers was the coming man. I listened with but half an ear as George, in the privacy of his home, berated everyone from grasping Scottish interlopers to simpering courtiers, calling them leeches, even heretics. Though I was startled by what followed.

''The Queen?' I asked, batting aside drowsiness that threatened. 'What of her?'

'I said, she is rumoured to have converted to Popery, and to go to confession regularly,' George replied sternly. 'Can you believe that?'

Having digested the notion, I made a sign of dismissal. 'Rumour's the bugbear of every age. Likely there's no foundation for it - James is a firm Protestant, as is his Danish queen-'

'I thought so, too,' George broke in sharply, 'as did everyone else. Until, that is, the viper Sarmiento arrived, and began to drip his poison in her ear.'

'Sarmiento…?'

'The Spanish ambassador.' George took a drink, then addressed me with some heat. 'That man's a silver-tongued *hidalgo*. In two years he's won the King's friendship with a blend of wit, coarseness and flattery – a master of the diplomatic arts, who knows precisely when and how to apply them. How else do you think the vile topic of a Spanish Match could even be broached?'

I fell silent. George's scathing tone, his evident outrage, surprised me somewhat: seldom had I heard him express his thoughts with such lack of restraint. Yet for all his faults he was a loyal subject, and as a man of firm principles was clearly dismayed by the state of affairs he observed. I glanced at Anne, who had lowered her eyes: no doubt the *topic* was only too familiar to her.

'A Spanish match,' I repeated, raking my mind for what I could recall of the matter, and finding nothing. 'Do you mean for the Prince Charles?' And when George barely nodded: 'But

I understood marriage negotiations with the French were still in progress.'

'Not for much longer,' George replied. 'Not since Sarmiento went to work on our sovereign, and little by little made him see the advantages of marrying his addle-pated son to the Infanta Maria Anna - who at nine years of age is no doubt the boy's equal in wit, despite his sixteen years. The primary advantage being a dowry of half a million pounds – you can see why the King is tempted.'

'I can,' I said, 'yet I doubt such a plan could be brought to fruition. The Privy Council, let alone the populace, would find it intolerable. To marry the heir to the throne to the daughter of our old enemy-'

'Quite so, Master Justice,' George interrupted; he too was apt to use my old form of address when he forgot himself. 'But you forget the sobriquet our sovereign likes: that of *Rex Pacificus* - the peacemaker king. It's almost twelve years since the treaty with Spain was signed... the unthinkable may become thinkable. Much has changed since you lived in London – more, I perceive, than you imagine.'

'So it would appear,' I said ruefully. 'I'm most grateful for the lesson.'

George paused, and seeing the look on Anne's face, had the grace to rein himself in a little. 'Your pardon, sir,' he said, 'if in my displeasure, I have allowed my heart to over-rule my head.'

'No...' I met his eye. 'You are righteous in your anger. I was unaware that the matter had grown as you describe. And yet I cannot believe our King would agree to Spanish terms for a marriage – he's no dullard, whatever men say. To begin with, would King Philip not insist that his daughter keep to her religion and be allowed to worship at will, with her own priests in attendance?'

'Of course - but that isn't all,' George answered, growing heated again. 'Not even the half of it. From what I know, the Prince would have to convert to her faith - do you not see? England would be ruled by Papists – in effect by Spain itself!'

I admit to being shocked by that notion. An old spectre rose unbidden, from a time I did not remember, but which was talked of constantly in my childhood: the five years' reign of Mary Tudor, when England answered to Rome and protestant martyrs burned to death in their hundreds. When Mary took her Spanish husband and would have made us vassals of Spain, had not Providence intervened by failing to provide her with a child – and by sending her to an early grave. In consternation, I turned the matter about.

'But surely the King's most trusted men have argued against it?' I protested. 'It would be intolerable to the Puritans on the Council.' And though George winced at the term, I lifted a hand.

'I mean no offence,' I said. 'And I share your disquiet. You understand me: men like the Earl of Pembroke, not to say Sir Ralph Winwood – the Secretary himself. They would not countenance such a marriage, whatever Sarmiento says - I cannot believe it will take place.'

George did not gainsay me immediately. His anger, though far from spent, subsided somewhat, so that he merely looked tired. 'As I told you, sir,' he said, 'much has changed in the last few years. Winwood is still Secretary of State, and an able man, but his influence is waning. As for his fellow Secretary, Sir Thomas Lake...' he grimaced as if the very name were distasteful. 'I'd not give a fig for his counsel. Did you know that he's a Papist in secret?'

'I did not,' I said, startled by the news.

'A jumped-up fellow of mean birth, who hunts with the King and talks bawdy to him – just the sort of company His Majesty enjoys. Lake lives close to the ambassador's house – they say he goes to mass there.'

'They also say his wife's a termagant, who beats him,' Anne said mildly.

'Perhaps she has good cause,' I said, thinking to lighten the discourse. But George was in earnest, and not to be diverted.

'Make no mistake, Popery is gaining ground in England,' he persisted. 'There are said to be more Jesuits in the country than ever before... some priests even saying mass openly, so I've heard. Where's the remedy – can you tell me?'

I gave no answer. On a sudden I thought of the Biershaws in their poverty, and Jane Rudlin too; to my mind, for most of His

Majesty's Catholic subjects little had changed. As for the Jessops: I caught Anne's eye and saw a trace of alarm, whereupon I sought to reassure her with my gaze. My wits were not so dulled as to let that business slip out. We were quiet for a while, until to my shame I yawned, and was at pains to stifle it. George, however, refrained from taking offence.

'Your pardon, sir; the candles are low, and doubtless you've heard enough of my prating,' he murmured, with an effort at humility. 'Can we spare you a ride back to Ludgate in the dark, and offer you a bed for the night?'

My response was a smile, which I hoped appeared as one of gratitude rather than mere relief.

I took farewell of Anne in the morning, after I had saddled Leucippus myself and led him from George's small stable to the house door. George was already up and gone, to some business which would not wait. My daughter stood in the chill with her mantle wrapped about her, Kate by her side. Having kissed them both I made ready to mount, promising to visit again before I left London. From the saddle I surveyed them briefly; and though my heart was heavy, I summoned a smile and a wave, and shook the reins.

My intention was to return to the inn, then to proceed with the business of finding the whereabouts of Jenner, the Master of Bedlam. Then I remembered what Jane Rudlin had said the day before, about a man named Elms who knew Thomas Jessop, and who kept a fencing hall in Aldersgate Street; if I passed through Islington and thence down Goswell Road, it was but a short ride. Within the half hour I was walking my horse along the busy thoroughfare, crossing Long Lane and mingling with the press of people heading into the city. Two enquiries of passers-by were enough to direct me to the fencers' hall: a narrow-fronted house with a painted sign of crossed swords. Finding a boy to hold Leucippus, I gave him a halfpenny and promised another on my return.

Since the door was unlocked, I entered and found myself in a surprisingly long room that extended back by means, I observed, of a yard that had been built over. The place resembled an armoury, being hung with enough swords to supply an entire company: tucks, rapiers and foils, even a Moorish blade that served, I supposed, merely for ornament. The floor was boarded and bare, with a large circle marked out in chalk. At the rear two young men were practising their swordplay, watched over by a big man in a buff leather coat, over which was a steel cuirass. As I came in he turned about, then strode towards me with a look which I read plainly: what in God's name was a man of my age doing here?

'Good day, sir… how may I aid you?'

The ex-soldier - for there was no mistaking it – eyed me shrewdly, taking in my station at a glance along, no doubt, with my poor physique. Here was a fighting man down to his bootheels, scars and all, with a hard eye and a thick beard; another casualty of the King's Peace, I judged, with nothing to sell but his swordsmanship.

'Master Elms? Richard Elms?'

'It is. And who am I addressing?'

I told him, and seeing he was not a man to waste time, I explained the reason for my visit briefly, to which his response was mild surprise. Yes, he knew Philip Mayne and liked him, he said. Though the boy lacked discipline and control, qualities vital to a swordsman. Was I a friend of his? And when I replied that I was:

'Where is he, then? I've not seen him in months… he was here often, in the autumn. Not sick, I hope?'

'In truth, he is unwell,' I answered, thinking how to lay out the matter; 'and his memory is cloudy. It would help me if you could tell what you know of him.'

A frown appeared. 'There's little to tell. He first came in… October, if I recall aright. Most keen to improve his fencing, he said - though from what I saw there was precious little to improve upon. But I taught him what I could, and he tried. Always courteous, and paid prompt. As I said, I liked him.'

'Did he say why he wished to learn swordplay?' I asked.

'No.'

The reply was deliberately abrupt, and not to be challenged.

Elms glanced over his shoulder to remind me that he had pupils to attend, then faced me again and waited. When I too waited, he made no secret of his impatience.

'It's not my custom to ask a fellow what brings him here,' he said. 'Besides, every man should know how to defend himself.' He gestured briefly to my basket-hilt rapier. 'I'll wager you wielded a blade, in your day.'

'A long time ago,' I told him. Unwilling to take my leave so soon, I asked him if he had served in the Dutch War, and received a curt nod of assent.

'I was at Sluis, and the Siege of Ostend... served under Ogilvie.'

'And after the Treaty?'

'I stayed for another five years.' Elms was frowning now. 'As a mercenary, sir, as you've likely surmised. What other trade is open to men like me, who know only soldiering? To some of us the Dutch Truce was just another bout of peace, that broke out like a whoreson rash.'

'And yet, you appear to have used your skills to good profit here,' I observed.

'I thank you,' came the tart reply. 'Now I must to my work.' With a final nod, he turned his back and strode away.

Outside, after paying off my horse-holder, I stood beside Leucippus and thought on what I had gleaned, little though it was; if anything, Thomas Jessop's actions since arriving in London made even less sense to me. Though the question that still troubled me most was: whence came the money he seemed to possess, in such abundance? Which led me back to the vexed matter of who was paying for his keep in Bedlam; and the only way to resolve that was by confronting its keeper.

I rode back to the Bel Savage, entrusted Leucippus to the same talkative ostler and went up to my chamber. Here I wrote a letter to Hester, telling her that I was uncertain when I would return home. After finding a boy and paying him to have it despatched, I pondered the notion of making another visit to Thomas, if with small hope of success. Besides, noon was approaching; it might be best to put it off until the morrow. I was about to return to my chamber, when I was accosted at the foot of the stairs by one of the inn's servants.

'There's a gentleman asking for you, sir. He's been already, and is come again.'

'Did he give a name?'

'He did not, sir, but he waits by the entrance. Will you receive him?'

'I'll go to him,' I said. My curiosity aroused, I walked down the passage and out by the street doors into the din of Ludgate Hill – and stopped.

'Belstrang! Is it truly yourself, after so long? I'd begun to think you were dead.'

For a brief moment I failed to recognise the imposing man who stood there, hatted and cloaked, a broad smile on his face. Then:

'Anstis?'

'Himself.' A hand flew out, to grasp mine. 'Are you well, sir?'

'I am… are you?' Mightily surprised by the meeting, I looked him over: Edmund Anstis, lawyer, whose face had once been familiar. Despite the passing of more than a decade since we'd met, the man was all but unchanged: handsome, impeccably groomed and barbered, the sharp eyes flitting across my features. Memories crowded in: of lengthy debates, as well as of raucous tavern nights. More than a dozen years my junior, the man was as alert and quick-witted as any I've known – and as sharp an opponent, too.

'You've confounded me,' I said at last. 'I've seen none of my old acquaintances, having been here but a few days.'

'Tut, Belstrang…' Anstis's expression changed to one of reproach. 'You belittle yourself, as always. I heard of your arrival yesterday, and would have taken you to supper, but it seems you slept elsewhere. Not between the sheets of an old friend of the other sex, I assume – or perhaps I shouldn't. A man's never too old, is he?'

'I was at the house of my daughter, Mistress Bull,' I said, somewhat sharply; the man's lewd tone irked me. Though when I recalled his reputation, I should not have been surprised: it was well known that, despite his good fortune in being married to a most attractive wife, Anstis generally frequented the Bankside Stews as much as the courts of law. His response was a yelp of laughter.

'A jest, Belstrang – come, are you such a provincial now? You've been too long in the country. And in truth, I recall your delightful Anne very well. I see her husband on occasions; a dry and brittle man, I fear….' He paused, took in my demeanour at a glance, and patted me on the arm in brotherly fashion.

'Pardon me, my old friend… your humours and mine were often at odds. This is no place for exchanging news – I came to invite you to take dinner with me. You've not lost your liking for good food and wine, I hope?'

'I have not,' I allowed, taken aback. 'Though I fear I've little news that would interest a townsman such as yourself. Will you join me here, at the inn?'

'By God, are you in earnest?' Anstis wore a look of mock horror. 'I wouldn't serve the Bel Savage's fare to my horse - I wonder you can bear the place. I had in mind the Irish Boy in the Strand, where I've bespoken a booth. Are you content?'

'Well, I suppose I should be,' I answered, reining in my dislike of the man's presumption; then, for all his faults, Anstis had always been good company. Soon we were making our way on foot through the bustle of Fleet Street, walking by the Temple, until after passing through the Bars we fetched up at the Irish Boy: a large inn that, as I recalled, had once been a known haunt of Papists. Guided by my companion, I was brought to a private corner booth where a jug of wine was promptly delivered. Anstis, with the natural air of a practised host, at once filled my cup. I tried the wine and found it excellent.

'Hippocras… as good as any I've tasted,' I said with approval.

Anstis wore his broad smile. 'Good… I trust the food will match it.'

It did: one of the finest meals I had enjoyed, it must be said, in a long while. At Thirldon we always made do with plain fare unless we had company, which was rare enough. Here at the Irish Boy, it seemed, Anstis had spared no expense: rabbit and capons came well-sauced, while the beef was well-roasted and most palatable with mustard. There were dishes I barely touched: ox-tongue, oysters and sweetmeats. The Hippocras was soon drunk, and replaced with a good Burgundy. At length, when sugared almonds and other tempting sweets lay before me, I confessed I was sated, as well as beholden to my host for his generosity.

For such it was: a generosity that went far beyond what might be expected of a chance encounter with a man I had not seen in many years; nor indeed, when all is turned about, was Anstis a man I ever considered a close friend, if a friend at all. Had it not been for the wine, and my host's convivial talk, my suspicions might have been aroused sooner: *in primis* as to how he knew I was in London, and *secundus*, how he knew where I lodged. As it was, we passed a pleasant hour of gossip and little else - until the moment came when Anstis set aside his platter, rested upon his elbows and fixed me with a bland expression that caught me off my guard.

'Well, Master Justice - I use the term from courtesy, as befitting one who has held that exalted office. You've been most diligent in your enquiries since coming up to town, have you not?' And when I showed surprise at his manner, he raised his brows and added:

'I speak of your interest in a poor, distracted papist - one Thomas Jessop. What in God's name, I wonder, do you want with him?'

SEVEN

The next hour or so, in which Edmund Anstis revealed his true reason for inviting me to such a sumptuous dinner, proved difficult. Filled with good food, my senses dulled with wine – as my host, of course, intended - I was in a poor condition to match wits with such a man. Yet by the end of our discourse much was changed, for in attempting to influence me as he did, he made an error: he had, it seemed, overlooked my innate stubbornness, carried through generations of Belstrangs. I might even say that his attempt to dissuade me from my purpose was a failure, in that it achieved its precise opposite.

It did not seem so at first. Having considered his question, which I saw was intended to throw me off-balance, I placed my arms on the table and met his gaze.

'Well now, what comes first to my mind,' I said, 'is to wonder of what possible interest my actions might be to you. Not to say, how you even knew I was come to London, let alone whom I might have visited.'

But on those questions Anstis was evasive. 'You've been seen, Belstrang - does it matter by whom? You were once a familiar enough sight about the Western suburbs. As to my own interest, you may consider it a concern for your welfare.'

At that I felt a prickling at my neck, and tried to shake myself out of the drowsy contentment into which I had lapsed. I did not forget that Anstis was a man who chose his clients from among those with the deepest pockets, and dispensed his concern for their welfare accordingly. In short, though he was smiling again, I detected the clear presence of a threat. Making no reply, I waited.

'To return to the subject of young Master Jessop,' he went on, 'it surprises me that you trouble yourself with him: a papist, the son of a known recusant, and a madman - a most pitiful one. Would it not be best to leave the poor wretch alone?'

'I'll repeat my question,' I said. 'Of what concern is this matter to you?'

'Then I too will repeat myself,' came the reply. 'It's you I'm thinking of, Belstrang, not Jessop. You do yourself no good in taking up his case.'

'His case?' I made a show of pondering the matter. 'Well now, if such exists, as a man of the law how would you adjudge his chances?'

'As a man of the law, I'd say they were non-existent.'

The answer came rapidly, as Anstis's smile faded. 'And let me say again, you are ill-advised to meddle in his business. My advice – gratis, of course – is to forget that wretched Bedlamite and return to Worcestershire.' He paused, then: 'A beautiful county, so I've heard from judges who travel the Circuit. I wonder you can bear the reek of London - it's become an anthill; or a midden, that stinks from Newgate to Aldgate. Westminster's little better - and people wonder why the King takes himself off at every opportunity to go hunting. What man wouldn't do so, if he could?'

I had to admire Anstis's way of turning the conversation; a casual listener might indeed think it was my welfare that concerned him – even that he spoke in earnest. But he had always been a slippery fellow; and more, I now knew without any doubt that I was being warned off, which showed a lack of judgement on his part. Perhaps he thought I was in my dotage, or close to it; perhaps he had forgotten my weakness, as some saw it, for pitying the helpless. Clearly he was not aware of how he had angered me, by thinking to play upon my senses as he did; as he also failed to realise how he had pricked my curiosity.

'True enough', I allowed. 'And there are many kinds of hunting... I enjoy pursuing a puzzle myself, until I can ferret out an answer.'

Anstis appeared not to have heard. He took a sip of wine, set it down and spoke without looking at me. 'I also heard you've been visiting a Mistress Rudlin, in Grays Inn Lane. That, too, was most unwise.'

I stared at him. 'By the heavens,' I exclaimed. 'Do you tell me that I'm being watched?'

'No - but she is.'

He raised his eyes, and I saw only coldness in his gaze. 'You must know who that woman is,' he said; then doubt appeared. 'Or, can it be that you don't?'

'Perhaps you'd care to enlighten me,' I said, tiring of this rigmarole. 'For I only know that she's a widow, who teaches children their letters.'

'Indeed?' Anstis paused again, then: 'You had no inkling that she was once the mistress of Thomas Percy, one of the Powder Treason plotters?'

'No... I did not.'

I was still, the news having sobered me in an instant: Thomas Percy, one of the prime movers of the great plot of 1605 - killed at Holbeach alongside the arch-plotter Catesby, where they had made their last stand. A kinsman to the great Earl of Northumberland, who languished in the Tower still, though he likely had no knowledge of the scheme... and Jane Rudlin, I now learned, had been Percy's mistress?

'Well now...' Anstis watched me closely. 'I perceive the news has come as a surprise to you. I might even say it's your good fortune that it's I who break it to you, and no other.' A trace of a smile appeared, as he nodded towards my cup. 'If you wish to know more, I'd fortify yourself, if I were you.'

'I'll forgo that pleasure,' I said, a trifle harshly. 'But pray, continue.'

'Very well...' he drew breath, and laid it forth. 'All the Powder Widows are watched; why would they not be, for who knows what mischiefs they may be party to? Percy had a wife, and children; his widow is paid a pension of fifty pounds a year by the papist Lord Monteagle. Mistress Rudlin, though no relation, receives ten pounds a year from Viscount Montague – another papist, for whom the most famous plotter of all once worked as a footman. I speak of the Yorkshireman, Fawkes. Now, do you see what sort of ground you've been treading?'

I made no answer. My senses swirling, I thought over my actions of the last few days, but could find little fault with them. What disturbed me was the notion that the prim, dignified woman with the silent daughter, who had befriended Thomas Jessop as a young fellow-Catholic in need of shelter, was other than what she seemed. I had suspected she knew more than she told, and yet…

'You understand me, I think,' Anstis resumed. 'The Crown can never rest in the matter of its Papist subjects – year on year come rumours of more plots. When the stables burned down at Farnham Castle, say, while the King was on Progress there, it had to be another attempt upon his royal person - naught to do with the groom who was careless with a candle. It's small wonder His Majesty's a nervous man who shuns crowds - so would I be, if I were him.'

'I'll admit that I haven't thought on such matters for a long while,' I said at last. 'Then, as you observed earlier, I'm but a provincial man. And I've not set eyes on the King, ever.'

'Have you not?' Anstis said, in a conversational tone. 'The first time I saw the King he was standing up to his bare ankles in blood. It's his cure for gout: to step into the warm carcase of a fresh-killed stag or buck, sometimes plunging his hands into it. He scoffs, so I heard, at those of a delicate nature who shy away from the practice. Then, he's a coarse man underneath his learning – one who wears majesty like an ill-fitting suit of clothes.'

I was confounded; Anstis's words could have amounted to treason. And I wondered at his purpose: was it to make me his confidant, or merely to put me further off my guard? I decided to make bold, and to challenge him directly.

'From what you say, do I now take it that you work for the Crown yourself?'

'I?' Anstis put on an innocent look that would have shamed a comedian. 'God's breath, Belstrang, what makes you think so? Moreover, even if I did, would I admit it to you, who consort with Papists? Let me say it again: this discourse of ours was but to give fair warning to a gentleman, and a man of the law like myself. Let me be charitable, and assume you've simply blundered into a matter unbefitting one of your status. As for your reputation…' He waited purposefully, and there was no mistaking the malice in his eyes as he delivered his final stroke.

'I fear your reputation, Belstrang, would be insufficient to the day, were you to find yourself facing questions from someone in higher authority. Your loss of the honourable position of Justice up at Worcester, and the careless manner in which you made enemies at the Quarter Sessions, have not passed unnoticed here. For the last time, I freely tend my advice: leave the matter of Thomas Jessop, forgo the company of the likes of Mistress Rudlin, and return to the bucolic charms of your county. There now, I'm ended: *satis*.'

And *satis* it was, for myself too. Without further words I rose from my seat and looked down at my host. I was angry, and curbing it with difficulty

'I don't know whose employ you are in, Anstis,' I said. 'But I ask you to give them my response to the advice you've dispensed - I'll not say the instructions. My business is my own, which I'll pursue in accordance with my own judgement and no-one else's. Only when it's concluded will I get myself out of this midden, as you term it, and take the westward road. Until then, my thanks for an excellent dinner – and a most informative one. Now I'll take my farewell.'

Which I did, mustering what dignity I could: striding out into the Strand with its rattle of wheels and hooves on cobbles, and the cracks of the carriers' whips, and into the rain that was falling. Head down I dove into the downpour, back towards the Fleet Bridge and the comfort of my inn-room. Only when I had arrived there, I knew, would I be able to order my thoughts; and only there could I be certain that I was not being watched.

The remainder of that afternoon passed quickly. Pacing the inn chamber while rain lashed the casement, I turned over the substance of my dinner with Anstis, and came to the edge of my knowledge. What had started with a half-hearted mission to find John Jessop's son was turning into something far murkier; and in my anger at the way in which Anstis delivered his warning, I was greatly unsettled. I had indeed consorted with papists: the Biershaws, who to my mind posed no threat to anybody; and Jane Rudlin who, it seemed, just might. Whereupon, dismissing the risks of such a course, I decided I would meet with the woman again, and force her to speak. For by instinct, and little else, I surmised there was more she could tell me about Thomas

Jessop; beyond that, her tale was of no interest to me. Or so I convinced myself, while unable to escape the knowledge that, for all her sobriety and devoutness, she had once been the mistress of a would-be regicide, whose head had been impaled on a pike above the south gate of London Bridge.

By the time evening came and the rain had passed, I was resolved to wait no longer.

Writing hurriedly by candlelight, I penned a short message telling the woman to repair to the Bel Savage within the hour, or I would come to her house and bring pursuivants with me: the charge would be concealing the whereabouts of a Catholic priest, and attending mass. It was a cruel threat, but I knew it would compel her to do my bidding, for the price of such a crime was heavier than she could bear. Having sealed the letter, I called a servant and paid him to take it to the house of Mistress Rudlin in Portpoole. He should wait while she read it, then escort her safely here, lighting the way with a link; no other action, I told him, would be accepted. As an afterthought, I paid him more to lead his charge by back ways to ensure they were not followed; if he suspected they were, he should double back until he was certain he had shaken off any pursuers. Having seen him away, I ordered a mug of spiced ale to warm my vitals, and settled down to wait.

Yet she did not come within the hour; nor within two hours.

The night wore on, the inn was as noisy as ever, and my room was cold. Sitting wrapped in a coverlet by the window, cursing what I now feared might have been foolhardiness on my part, I thought to order a dish of hot coals and another mug. I yawned often, my belly still full from the dinner at the Irish Boy. I was on the point of taking to my bed and propping myself with pillows, when at last came a repeated knocking at the door, soft but insistent. At once I was on my feet, hastening to open it and finding myself facing the servant I had hired, now sour-faced and in something of a sweat.

'Your pardon, sir,' he muttered. 'But I've been sorely pressed – she's not a woman to be hurried. What with finding a neighbour to mind her daughter, and waiting while she dressed herself; not to say wandering the lanes of Clerkenwell, walking by Smithfield and Old Bailey and stopping every minute to let her catch up - in truth I'm fucking done for, and that's the whole of it.'

'Watch your tongue,' I told him. 'Is she here, or not? And if not…'

I broke off as Jane Rudlin herself stepped into view, wrapped in a heavy cloak with a hood, eying me in silent resentment. Standing aside, I let her enter the room, then with a glance at the servant, who was clearly hoping for further payment, I closed the door.

She would not sit, and kept her cloak on, throwing back the hood. Standing by the window, looking down upon the inn-yard where lights burned, she said not a word. When I asked if she would take a drink to warm herself, she merely shook her head. So I brought stools to the window and seated myself, letting her stand if she would.

'I've learned a good deal about you since we last met, mistress,' I said by way of a beginning. 'Tell me, is your daughter the child of Thomas Percy?'

She whirled round to face me, and I saw the depths of her anger. 'If you know it already, then why do you ask?' She demanded. 'And more, what matters it to you who her father is?'

'Very likely it does not,' I answered. 'Yet I've a notion that you haven't been forthright with me - and I suspect you know more about Thomas Jessop's affairs than you revealed. For one thing, you read his last letter, yet you swore you knew nothing of this blow he spoke of: *a blow for all those of our benighted faith*, if I recall his words correctly. Which category, of course, includes yourself.'

She was tense as a wand, well aware of the danger she could be in from one who, as a former Justice, had easy recourse to the law. But the look that came over her face now, was of a different nature. Gazing down at me, she gestured towards the four-poster bed which half-filled the chamber.

'So, you must think you have me at your mercy, sir,' she said in a voice of contempt. 'Is this your price, for leaving me alone?

Believe me, you would not be the first man to use his power in such a way.'

I gave a start: in what I must call my naivety, I had not foreseen how my action in forcing her here could be interpreted. I shook my head, my expression causing her to frown.

'By all that's holy, madam,' I exclaimed, 'I had no such intent, nor do I yet! I want naught but answers from you - which thus far have been few enough. And more,' I added indignantly, 'you appear to have formed a very ill opinion of me. I suggest you ask my pardon, whereupon we might put this error of judgement aside and converse in a proper manner.'

She was quiet then, looking intently at me until her angry frown faded. Lowering her eyes, she murmured something I failed to catch; it sounded like a fragment of Latin. At last she looked up and said: 'If I've done you wrong, sir, I do ask pardon - with all my heart. You've little knowledge of what my life has been, these past ten years and more – then, why should it be otherwise? You and I are as two islands, visible to one another across an impassable channel.'

'Perhaps so,' I allowed, letting out a breath. 'But will you please sit? Or I shall get a sore neck, looking up at you.'

She sat down, doubtless gladly enough after her long walk, and gathered her cloak about her. 'I know why your servant brought me by roundabout ways,' she said, after a pause. 'All those who had even the least connection with the Powder Treason are watched, as they are despised. Despite the fact that, had they known the extent of it beforehand, most would have recoiled with horror from such an action.'

'So I've heard,' I said somewhat sharply, 'but I've no wish to delve into that business – nor to know more of your relations with one of its plotters. I want to know all that you know of Thomas Jessop, particularly in those days before he was taken off to Bridewell. Once again, I assure you your testimony will remain private between us. You may believe me, or not – it doesn't trouble me unduly.'

She hesitated; then, as I had observed once before, the fight seemed to go out of the woman. She was tired and weighted down with worry, but after a while she spoke.

'Thomas never told me what he intended, but since then I've suspected what it was - and it fills me with dread. I once thought he was deluded, until I learned he had been to see a priest to ask his blessing for his venture.' She stiffened. 'Please don't ask me the priest's name. I beg you, as I begged you before-'

'That's of no concern to me,' I said, brushing the matter aside. 'You say you had suspicions about this venture – what were they?' And when she still seemed reluctant, I raised my hand and pointed a finger at her. 'You cannot stop now. Tell me all, or I'll carry out my threat - and to the devil with my promise of secrecy!'

She blanched, bringing her hands together; for a moment I thought she meant to pray, but instead she gripped herself tightly, twisting her fingers; she was in turmoil. But at last she sighed, and said:

'You recall those words in his letter… when he urged his father to mind the words of De Talavera?'

'I do, though the name means nothing. Who is that?'

'Juan de Talavera… a Spanish Jesuit,' came the reply. 'He wrote that it's lawful to kill a tyrant.'

I gazed at her; then I shuddered, and not merely from the chill of the room. The truth came barrelling at me, bringing mayhem in its wake: a truth that, I saw at once, had been lying just beyond my comprehension for the past day or so – perhaps longer. I saw the fear in Jane Rudlin's eyes, as I recalled the cold look on the face of Edmund Anstis, as he spoke of plots and machinations…

'You mean, as Fawkes and the others claimed?' I said, aghast. 'That they had the right –'

I broke off and drew breath, berating myself for a fool whose wits were as dull as any Bedlamite. 'The anniversary,' I said, my eyes on the floor as I pieced it out. 'The fifth of November, last year… ten years since the Powder Plot.'

She barely nodded. 'I believe now that Thomas meant to avenge those men, who were thwarted in their actions and brought to such a terrible death. That was his purpose, in the carrying out of which he was ready to die; though I swear to you, sir, as God is my witness, that he did not confide in me.'

Chilled by her words, I stared in silence.

'I've thought on it since,' she continued, 'and now I believe that's why he went to Elms to learn to wield a sword. He was fierce in those last days – feverish, with a zeal that troubled me; I've said he drank heavily, and would mutter to himself, so that I feared for his sanity. More, I feared for my daughter – I asked him to master himself, or forbear to come to our house again. But then he would ask my pardon most pitifully; he even kneeled before me, swearing his love for me, and for all those who bear the yoke for practising our faith. Then came that last day: the fifth of that month, when he lost his reason altogether, as I have told you. I can add little more, except...' she hesitated, then:

'Once, after he'd drunk too much, he said he would be the English Ravaillac.' Whereupon she bowed her head, and did not look up.

But I had heard enough, and was dismayed: Ravaillac, the papist fanatic who had killed King Henri of France in Paris six years before; who had been caught and tortured beyond endurance, his body pulled apart by horses... abruptly I rose from my seat and walked about the room. When I turned, Jane Rudlin was looking at me, her face in shadow.

'As you may know, sir,' she said quietly, 'the bishops preach an anniversary sermon each fifth of November before the King, to give thanks for his deliverance from the Plot. Last year at Whitehall, Bishop Andrews was the Anniversarist. And Thomas Jessop...'

'Thomas Jessop's intent was to be another kind of Anniversarist,' I finished.

'And now,' I went on, my mind leaping, 'I understand why you said all I could do was to pray for him as you did – as you do still. What is it you pray for – his early death, or for his soul, or both?'

She gave no answer, but looked away; while from the inn beneath us came a bellow of raucous laughter.

Utterly downcast, I sank on to my stool.

EIGHT

In fact, we talked more freely then, Jane Rudlin and I; now that the truth was out, there was small need for dissembling. For myself, I was in a quandary, my revulsion at the act Thomas Jessop had intended being tempered only by the knowledge that, for whatever reason, he had failed in his purpose. Moreover, it had been the undoing of him, driving him at last to madness – which, many would say, God had seen fit to visit upon him for his wickedness. What a papist-hating puritan like my son-in-law might say, I did not care to dwell on.

'Do you not know what a case you are in?' I demanded of her, once I had recovered my wits. 'If you had the least suspicion of what Thomas planned to do, you should have denounced him at once - by not doing so you made yourself an accessory to the fact. You could have been hanged at Tyburn, before a crowd that would bay and screech at you until your last breath… indeed, you could still-'

'I pray you, sir, enough!'

In anguish she faced me, shaking her head like one distracted. 'You've no need to make me a picture. Those who were wives of the conspirators - even less than a wife, as I was – know more of such dangers than you can imagine. Have I not lain awake at night in fear of my life – let alone that of my daughter?' On a sudden, the woman looked close to tears. 'When she stood in the market and watched a puppet show of the Powder Plot, cheering with others at the grisly death of Fawkes, what should I say to her? That her own father was one of those men? Could I tell her that I'd stood in the crowd on those two January days in 1606, just another shivering spectator, and watched those that were left put to the cruellest of deaths – their very innards burned before their eyes? Have I not prayed daily for God's mercy – and yes, confessed, until my soul was raw with remorse…'

She fell silent, looking down at her hands while she worked them. I was torn: between anger with this woman, for who she was and what she had concealed from me, and a grudging pity for her. I knew how the families of the dozen or so reckless papists who planned to kill the King had suffered: reviled, broken by their men's Treason, driven into hiding or exile, or simply shutting themselves in their homes to live as best they could. Only the widow of Sir Everard Digby it was said, being a Protestant, lived on in peace and comfort. Still on my feet, pacing the chamber in my agitation, I looked down at Jane Rudlin and tried to order my thoughts.

'Do I take it that Thomas knew who you were – who you are?' I asked her.

She shook her head. 'I do not know, for he never asked me anything about myself. He knew I was widowed, and of his faith, which seemed enough. As for whoever it was sent him to me, I swear I still have no knowledge of who that was, nor how much they knew about me.' She lowered her eyes again. 'The business is murky still, though with Thomas confined and silent, I hoped it was behind me. Yet now...'

'Now I've come to stir it all up again,' I finished. 'In God's name, mistress, would it not have been better if you'd told me everything from the start?' Whereupon I answered my own question. 'No... you did not know me, and had no reason to trust me. I'm no priest, to be bound by the ties of confession.'

We both lapsed into silence: as bleak a silence, in that cold room, as I have ever known. I was mighty tired of the day's revelations, while Jane Rudlin was in fear of what would follow. In truth I knew not how to proceed – unless it were possible to uncover the remainder of this fearful business, merely for my own peace of mind.

'Had you not thought what would happen if Thomas came to his senses in Bedlam, and told everything?' I asked at last. 'His very words, whether anyone believed them or not, would be enough to condemn him.'

'You may be certain I've thought on it, these past months – more times than I can count,' she answered. 'And yet...' she hesitated, then: 'For a while I had hopes that he had not lost all his senses; that he stayed silent to protect those who helped him

– not just myself and the Biershaws, but perhaps others too. Then at my last visit to him, as I told you, those hopes faded to nothing. He waits only for death, after which he will face his Maker, who will judge him as no mortal can.'

'And I?' I looked hard at her. 'Do you hope that I too will remain silent?'

She gave no answer, but I saw that she harboured no such expectation. Why would she, of a Protestant, a former magistrate and a loyal subject of the Crown? She expected no justice, for there would be none for a woman in her place. Hence my surprise, when she drew breath and said:

'Whatever you might say, Master Belstrang, I suspect it would not matter. For there's one thing more I will tell, which might alter your view.' And when I frowned, she went on: 'There are others who seem to know a good deal about Thomas and his actions – perhaps more than you and I put together. I speak not of neighbours, nor of the Biershaws...others who are less kind, I think.'

I gave a start then, as a name sprang to mind: Anstis, who had warned me that same afternoon that I should cease my enquiries and leave London. I waited.

'That same evening,' Jane Rudlin continued, 'after Thomas fell into frenzy and was taken to Bridewell, I was visited by two men I did not know. Not constables... men-at-arms, though without a livery. They pushed open the door to my house, putting me in great fear, and demanded I tell them where Thomas was. When I told what had occurred – that he'd been arrested and taken to Bridewell - they were very angry. I was ordered to send my daughter to bed, whereupon they put me against a wall, held a poniard to my neck and told me what I must do; if I failed...' she almost shuddered.

'I'll not relate what it was they promised to do – telling of it in the vilest language I ever heard - for it concerned not only me, but my daughter too. I believe a shrewd man like you might piece out the threat for yourself.'

'And what were their orders?' I asked, after a moment.

'Firstly, to forget that they had been here, and not speak of it to anyone. 'Secondly, never to try and look for Thomas, nor enquire about him. If I did so...' she closed her eyes, and ended: 'My life would be ruined.'

'And yet, when I first came to your house, you told me not only that he was alive, but where he was held,' I countered. 'You even went to visit him in Bedlam - why did you so?'

'In truth, I cannot tell why,' she answered, so quietly I could barely hear. 'Let me say only that a person to whom I went for succour gave me his counsel: that if Thomas's family came to seek for him I should tell them all I knew, and how they might retrieve his body for proper burial. They had that right – while I had none.'

Then at last she did weep, silently into her hands, turning away from me. I could only watch, and wonder at her tale. The person she had gone to was a priest, of course; had she told him of her suspicions as to what Thomas had planned to do, I supposed the man would be in fear – for himself, as much as for others. Whereupon, in her shame and fear, Jane Rudlin had tried to find a path through the mire she was in.

For all my scruples, I could not find it in my heart to condemn her.

'I will ask one more thing of you,' I said at last. 'Is there a part of you, however small, that wishes Thomas had succeeded in his plan to commit regicide? To kill King James, whom most people of your faith believe to be the cause of all their woes? Answer me.'

She removed her hands and looked up at me, her face wet with tears. 'In God's name, I abhor the notion, as would any Christian!' she exclaimed. 'Those men – and yes, the one who was my lover too – had crossed a line, into evil. Though I knew naught of it until later, for he had not sought my company in the months before. When I learned of it...' in despair, she hung her head.

'The Powder Treason was madness - and it still does its work, as the skulls of the perpetrators stand yet upon the Bridge. We shall never escape its shadow, as England celebrates its anniversary by statute, with bonfires in the streets. Only God can forgive them: Catesby and Rookwood, the Wintours and the Wrights, Fawkes and the rest - as only He can forgive Thomas, who sought to emulate them in his rage and his foolishness. That's where blind and boundless devotion can lead: to sainthood, or to devilry. May the Lord help him – and help all of us.'

She sagged then, as one who is spent, and I did not press her further. The hour was late; even the noise of the inn had subsided. For a while we sat, prey to our own thoughts: like two islands, as she had described it, within sight of one another yet each a stranger. At last I rose, wearied by the discourse, and said I would call a servant to light her homeward, which seemed to bring little comfort. She stood up, shivering in the cold room, and drew her cloak about her.

'What will you do, sir?' She asked, her eyes upon me. 'Now that I've told you what I know?'

'In truth, I've not the least notion,' I answered.

And a short time later, with barely a farewell, she was gone. Likely I will never set eyes on her again. My hope is that she thrives still, to teach children their letters.

Despite all that had occurred that day I did sleep, after some hours of trying. By the time I awoke the morning was well advanced, with weak sunlight showing at the casement – and at once events crowded in upon me, causing me to groan aloud. Low in spirits, I rose and went to the door, shouting for a footman to bring water for washing. When one came, I ordered him to send up bread and porridge, and honey, and a mug of beer to steady myself. After he was gone I sank down upon the bed, my thoughts a tangled web. What in God's name, I asked myself, had I stumbled into?

For in truth I was beside myself. To begin with, I could only imagine the grief that would be visited on John Jessop and his wife, should they learn what their son had intended: how he had deceived them, and why he had come to London. *Secundus*, I knew only too well what action the Crown authorities would take, were I to tell them what I knew. Thomas would be dragged from Bedlam and put to the most brutal kind of interrogation, which no man can stand for long. He would speak in the end – and yet, at the final turn whatever he said would make no difference: he was bound for execution, and all of London would rejoice to watch him die.

Yet another, even darker business lay behind the schemes of that deluded young man - of that I felt certain. There was the matter of the money he'd had about him, to spend freely, and the matter of who paid for his stay in Bedlam – not to say why they would do so. There was the vexed matter of Anstis with his false smile, telling me I was on dangerous ground, and should step back or face some unnamed consequence. It irked me still; and Jane Rudlin's testimony – which I now thought, despite her anguish, had afforded her some relief in sharing it with another – had put the matter in a different light. Hence my choice - as I had thought more than a week ago, when John Jessop came to me – was stark indeed, and caused me grave disquiet. I could give up the entire quest, consign Thomas to his fate, go back to Thirldon and try to forget, even if to do so were impossible. Then, such a course would also oblige me to lie to his father, telling him perhaps that Thomas refused to leave Bedlam, or that I was unable to secure his release - or even that he had died, as Jane Rudlin once urged me. Otherwise…

I stopped, sitting half-dressed in my chamber, and berated myself for a coward and a liar. How could I even contemplate such a notion? I saw John Jessop, in his grief and worry; I saw Hester, telling me how the man's poor wife was distracted; I even saw Childers with his dour face, and read his thoughts: *a gentleman does not stoop to chicanery, Master Justice…*

I cursed aloud then, as roundly as I'd done in years - because my choice was no choice at all: I must see the matter through, and find out who else was a party to this business. For it seemed plain enough that somebody was. Perhaps, I reasoned, Thomas had been persuaded by others: chosen as one angry or foolish enough - or both - to attempt the gravest of crimes. Perhaps he had confessed to one of his ilk, and found a co-conspirator with a little money to spare. And perhaps, on the brink of carrying out his plan – even on the very anniversary itself, he had at last come to his senses and seen what wickedness he was fallen into, which explained his losing his mind.

I sighed, daunted by the task that lay ahead. Who could I

confide in, who would not call me mad for what I did – who would not, in all likelihood, inform on me at once? Even George, my own kinsman, would recoil from me. The matter was beating upon me when there came a knock on the door, and a servant appeared with my breakfast. But the food was like ashes in my mouth; for some reason I thought of the gourmand, Colley Biershaw, who ate anything and, I supposed, cared not a jot how it tasted.

And yet in this Year of Astonishment even ex-Justice Belstrang, in his wildest fancies, never compassed how things would fall out on that day.

The morning was waning when I left the inn and walked round to the stables to see Leucippus. In the yard, three or four stable lads were gossiping and fooling, so that I was obliged to call one to order and demand that he find the ostler. The man came quickly, in his leather apron, and on recognising me made his bow. If I cared to come inside, I was told, I could view the horse myself and be assured that he had the best of care. I did so, and was content.

'What kind of a name is that, sir - Leucippus?' The ostler enquired, screwing up his eyes as he peered at me. 'I'll swear I never heard it before.'

'He was a philosopher... one of the ancients,' I told him absently; my mind was elsewhere. 'Some say he never existed, but I think differently.' I was on the point of leaving, whereupon the fellow was bold enough to catch my sleeve.

'Heard you had company yesternight, master,' he murmured, with a sly look. 'Also heard the lady left, a while later... not a full night's worth, then?'

'What?' I swung round at him, my anger rising. 'How dare you, fellow...'

'Peace, sir, I mean no insult – to the devil with me if I do.' He raised his hands, summoning a huckster's smile. 'I thought only... well... a man should not lie alone at night. If you'd place your trust in me, it would be my pleasure to supply your needs: a woman of the best quality to warm your bed - and to suit your tastes, whatever they might be.'

I regarded the man, who now wore an expectant smile, then reined in my indignation and sighed. What cause had I to berate him after all, who provided such a service? With a shake of my head, I turned and left the stables.

On re-entering the inn, I took a table by a window that overlooked Ludgate Hill and called for a cup of the best sack. I had formed no plan yet on how best to proceed, beyond seeking out Jenner, the master of Bedlam. The events of the day before weighed heavily upon me; in all honesty I had little appetite for braving this storm I was caught up in. I drank as the inn filled up about me, watching the traffic of foot and horse that flowed past the window. I was about to call for a second cup when a figure in rustling skirts appeared, and leaned over me.

'Here you are all alone, sir… and I'm right glad to see you. May I sit?'

I looked up into a whitened face, painted with cerise and surmounted by a copper-coloured periwig. The cherry-red gown was trimmed with lace and so low-cut that the breasts almost poked out at me, as doubtless their owner intended. Somewhat startled, I blinked twice, which caused the woman to chuckle.

'Your pardon, master… did I break your reverie?' She smiled. 'If you will accept my company, I can bring you joy enough to fill your dreams for a fortnight. I'm Mary Wedd – and you are Sir Robert?'

'I'm not *sir* anybody,' I said, finding my voice. 'And if you've been sent here by that rogue of an ostler, Mary Wedd, you can go and tell him I'm sorely displeased by his effrontery. You were misinformed, for I'll have nobody's company but my own. Kindly leave me be.'

To my displeasure, however, the woman showed not the least intention of complying. Instead she indicated an empty stool beside mine, and said: 'Can I not even rest my legs, sir? Surely you won't scorn to have my body beside yours?' Whereupon seeing my indignation rising anew, she changed tack.

'Then at the least buy me a mug, won't you, for charity's sake? I'd thank you heartily and be on my way, if that's your pleasure.' When I hesitated, she picked up my cup and looked inside it. 'Let me serve you with my own hand, sir... sack, is it?'

'Well... it is,' I said, somewhat shamed by my abject surrender. Then, why should I not accept this diversion? I asked myself. Though I had no intention of letting it go further than drinking with her, to forget my troubles for a while. It was many years since a young Robert Belstrang had sought the company of trulls, with all the risks that entailed; yet I reached for my purse, plucked out coins and bade her take my cup to the drawer to be refilled. Watching her move unhurriedly between the tables, with the eyes of many men following her as she went, I found a smile appearing, and suppressed it at once.

She returned with a cup in each hand, set them before us and sat down beside me, arranging her skirts. Without delay she lifted her drink in her fist and took a long pull, before lowering it with a smile of satisfaction.

'You've quite a thirst, Mary Wedd,' I remarked. 'Have you had a busy morning?'

'Well now, how should I answer that, good Master Robert?' came the reply. 'Yet I thank you most heartily for enquiring, as I do for your hospitality.'

I took up my own cup, saluted her with it and drank, somewhat ruefully. The ostler, it seemed, had chosen to take my lack of a spoken refusal for, in effect, a token of assent. But though it irked me, there was no harm done - or so I thought. Soon the woman was prating as to an old friend: of the rain that had soaked her two days before and ruined a rose-pink gown, of her sister who was struck down with a flux, and of a madman that was going about Paul's claiming he was the true son of Queen Elizabeth, and would have his rights. He was bound for Bedlam, that one; Mary Wedd was certain of it. Then, if some people had their way, half the King's Council would be there too – was it not the honest truth?

'No doubt many would concur with you,' I said, taking another drink. It was the first sentence I had uttered for some time, being distracted as I was, and glad enough to let her divert me with her chatter. Noon passed; I heard the bell clanging from St Bride's, just beyond the Fleet Bridge. Beyond lay Shoe Lane, and the Biershaws' house... a vague notion arose, that I might visit them and ask further about Thomas Jessop; then I remembered I had promised not to trouble them again - or had I? At once a cloud of doom fell upon me, as I thought again of Jane Rudlin's testimony, and how I might forge a path through what seemed like a dense forest...

I was frowning, gazing down at the table. About me the inn swirled like a fog, while the noise seemed to swell to a roar. My eyelids drooped... had I drunk so much, I wondered? Blearily I turned to Mary Wedd, who was smiling and nodding at me. But though her lips moved... swollen lips painted with vermilion, I saw as if for the first time... no sound emerged. Uneasily, I opened my mouth to speak, but only a croak came forth; there was a rushing in my ears - and the table tilted up towards me, striking my head with a thud; then, darkness.

When I awoke, I was in the Compter in Wood Street, imprisoned for debt.

NINE

The debt, I was informed by a turnkey, was for twenty-five pounds, to a gentleman whose name I knew; if I chose to insist that I did not know it, then it wasn't his place to tell me. This I learned as I sat on a hard bench in a tiny, dim room with two stone-faced ruffians standing over me, my head throbbing as if I'd been truncheoned.

'This is a most fearful mistake, and you shall soon know it,' I said feebly. From the poor light that came through the single, dirty window I divined it was late in the afternoon, though I had no memory of what had passed since noon. 'I'm Robert Belstrang of Thirldon, gentleman - and I've committed no offence, nor do I owe a debt to any man. I will have recourse to justice – you may rely upon it.'

My answer, however, was a snort of laughter.

'Justice? Well, you may have it in time – that and anything else you desire, if you can afford it,' one of them said. 'But first you pay garnish, before we let you leave this room. The charge is a shilling.'

Instinctively my hand went to my belt – whereupon I received a further shock. My purse was there, but it was very light indeed. More, my sword and poniard were gone, as were my rings - and only now did the gravity of my case strike home.

'By the Christ, I've been robbed!' I blurted.

'Is it so?' The bigger of the two turnkeys, who was built like a wrestler, gave me a disbelieving look. 'Best open up, then, and see if anything's left.'

Somewhat shakily, with troubled thoughts crowding my mind, I tugged open the purse and tipped the contents into my palm: two shillings, where earlier there had been ten pounds or more in gold and silver. In dismay I stared down at the coins, then flinched as a calloused hand was pointed at my chest.

'A shilling to pass from here, once we've entered your name in the book,' the turnkey said. 'Another sixpence will get you to the Two-penny Ward, and the remainder will buy you a mug and a half loaf. After that, master Belstrang, you must bear yourself as best you can.'

Horrified, I stared up at him; I well knew what he meant. A new arrival at the debtor's prison must part with money to obtain even the basest of comforts; if he has none he is a charity case, fit only to beg. Many starve, or fall sick, yet there is no mercy to be had in the Compter. Until a man can find some means of paying off his debt, he is caged like a rat.

'But this is intolerable,' I croaked; my mouth was as dry as sawdust. 'I've been cruelly used... I'm lodging at the Bel Savage, whose landlord will affirm it. In my chamber there's a cloak, a hat and other items worth twenty pounds at the least, and in the stable a horse worth fifty-'

I stopped: my tongue had run away from me, for whatever my plight, I knew I could not part with Leucippus. I coughed, and tried to gather myself.

'Well then, you've small need to worry,' the turnkey said. 'For a sixpence, you can send one to the inn to verify your tale, in which case the debt might be discharged. Though, I have to say that a man's possessions often fall short of achieving what he says they're worth, when offered at sale... is it not so?'

The question was addressed to the other turnkey, who nodded at once.

'It is,' he agreed. 'And more, the lackeys at the Bel Savage, I've heard said, may not scruple to filch from a man's chamber while he's absent. I'd not be surprised if your cloak and other stuffs were found to be missing, my friend, and that's the plain truth of it.'

The truth? In mounting dismay I looked into his pitiless face, then back to his companion, who could not help but smirk at me. I was powerless, I saw, and it was a sensation both strange and frightful to me: the former magistrate who had sent more men to the gaols than he could remember. I shook my head, trying to think, but the keepers had no patience left.

'Come, the hour grows late,' I was told. 'Pay the garnish and you may pass through the door, pay at the next one and you'll find somewhere to rest. I wager it won't be as fancy as you're used to, but you'll make the best of it.'

And so, to my utter wretchedness, I had no other course than to obey. Head down, overcome with shame at the indignity of it, I gave up my shilling and allowed myself to be marched like a felon from the ante-room, past a door studded with square-headed nails into a foul-smelling passage lit by a single lantern. Here I was delivered to another turnkey, a swag-bellied fellow who demanded my remaining shilling. When I protested that I'd been told the fee was sixpence, I was cut short in an instant.

'A shilling, or you sleep here on the stones,' the man grunted.

Well, I paid again - and for the first time in my life found myself penniless.

Shuffling through another door, my throat parched and my head still aching, I was let into a large, malodorous room full of people, some of whom turned to look at the new arrival. Whose only error, I knew now, had been to let a harlot serve him a cup of sack in which a sleeping potion had been mixed.

Between clenched teeth I cursed Mary Wedd, with her broad smile and her copper-coloured periwig, to the very devil.

Thereafter Robert Belstrang passed his first night in the Wood Street Compter, which as London's prisons go is not the worst. Nor was it the worst night I have ever known: the one on which Margaret died must claim that prize. Yet it was, shall I say, among the most miserable. Despite my condition I slept not a moment, spending the whole time crouched in a corner, regarding my fellow prisoners as potential assailants who would likely overpower me and strip me bare. Yet in that regard I was in error, for none approached me; not even when, towards dawn, I dozed from sheer weariness, to awake with a start and wonder in God's name where I was. When the memories rose I let out a great sigh, along with a groan.

'Might I ask you your name, sir?'

I turned sharply, to face a remarkably well-dressed man in a good slashed doublet open at the neck, seated beside me. On recognising him as a gentleman like myself, I must have showed such surprise that he laughed.

'Mine is Curriter, from Loughton in Essex,' he informed me. 'I'll guess the misfortune that's brought you here is similar to mine – a matter of debt?'

'It's false,' I muttered, then broke into a cough; my throat was raw still. To my further surprise, Curriter produced a leather horseman's flask and offered it.

'It's weak beer, and not of the best... all I can get now,' he said. 'Yet you're welcome to a little of it.'

I accepted and drank, as sparingly as I could. 'I'm... my name's Robert,' I told him as I returned the flask, 'and I thank you with all my heart.'

'Well, Robert, you are in a pickle,' my companion said amiably. 'Had you not enough money about you to get into the Knight's Ward, nor even the Master's?'

'I had not,' I answered. I knew what he spoke of: those with a full purse might buy the best the Counter had to offer, extending to a room of their own with a bed, food and wine brought in; even, I've heard, women of the streets to warm them at night... whereupon a most fearful thought struck me.

'And I see now, that whoever it was who contrived to get me sent me here was most careful in that respect,' I went on, in mounting dismay. 'In short, there was just enough remaining in my purse to bring me to where I am now, and not a penny more.'

Curriter showed passing interest. 'You mean, the man to whom you're indebted?'

'There is no such person,' I began – then pulled myself up short. I had no stomach, I realised, for telling my tale; nor would my case arouse sympathy here. Doubtless many in the Counter would claim to have been wronged in some way. As for giving my true name and station, that would be foolhardy indeed: on learning that I'd once been a man of the law some might have beaten me, or worse.

'No such person?' Curriter repeated, raising his brows at me. 'Then what have you done – or should I ask, whom have you offended?'

I had no answer. With a heavy heart I looked about me, at the wretches with whom I now shared a living space: as pitiful a body of men and women as could be imagined. Some were silent, sitting alone in their misery; others were busy in conversation, even near to coming to blows. Still others appeared to be ill, coughing and gagging most unpleasantly. Moreover, Curriter and I were watched, I saw, by at least one man whom I would not dare to confront. And yet, as gentlemen, we two were far from being alone in our station: I saw others in dirty and bedraggled clothing that had once been of good quality, and another in a skull cap and threadbare black gown. When I caught his eye, the man nodded at me.

'That's the quacksalver,' Curriter informed me. 'I call him the *mirum vincularum*: the wonder of the prison. He can cure anything from the French pox to a head-cold - or so he'll tell you, and his charges are most reasonable. Unfortunately, his skills don't seem to extend to curing the Spanish fever that's crept in. Then, I mean to escape it, for I'll be gone by this afternoon.'

'You're leaving?' I asked, attempting to absorb all that he'd said.

'Indeed – my debt will be paid in full by a friend of mine, now that it's safe for me to go out. The man I was hiding from has given up the case and gone back to the country, I hear - the best news I've had in a month.'

Not understanding, I stared at him. 'You've been hiding here for a month...?'

'Almost,' my fellow-prisoner replied. 'I got myself committed, just in time; the one I lost to at cards is not a man of scruples. I'd barely an hour to gather enough money to pay for my board. It ran out yesterday... the beer you tasted is all I have left.' Seeing my expression he gave another laugh, though not unkindly.

'You're clearly a novice here, Robert,' he went on. 'Hence, I advise you to summon every scrap of your wits, and to learn quickly. You must find a way to trade, or you'll go hungry - or more likely you'll catch the fever first. Look about you, and note the ones to keep away from.'

'But this is terrible,' I said, in mingled dismay and disbelief. 'Do you tell me there's a sickness here, and no-one does anything to remedy it?'

'What would you have them do, empty the prison?' Curriter asked. 'You'll have met the sort of men who are our keepers -

do you think they'd care if we all perished, so long as they don't catch it? Were Newgate or The Fleet emptied, when the plague struck London?'

I was dumbstruck; despite what I thought I knew of London's gaols, never had I experienced such cruel indifference to suffering. I brooded on what Curriter had told me, and on the desperate condition to which I'd been brought – then, on a sudden, the truth came at me in a blinding flash.

'Good God,' I muttered. 'This is deliberate... I've been put here to die.'

'Do you believe so?' Curriter raised his brows. 'Then you must have greatly offended someone – one with influence, I'd guess.'

'I must think,' I told him, struggling to do so. 'There are men I might call on would get me out of here, if I can get a message to them...'

'That's wise,' my companion said. 'And I would call on them as soon as you can, otherwise you'll fall victim to this fever.' He pointed across the room, to a figure lying along the wall. 'It starts with catarrh, and a fearful sweating - don't let any of those afflicted near you. As for getting a message out, it can be done with ease if you have the money. You can even pay one of the turnkeys to take you out for an hour, to conduct your business.'

'But I have nothing,' I said. 'They took my money, and everything of value...' I looked down forlornly at my good breeches and doublet, already begrimed and dusty. 'Unless I undress myself down to shirt and hose...'

'I doubt that would suffice,' Curriter said, with a shake of his head. 'They get offered all kinds of frippery – not that your clothes are cheap, of course. But if you had a chain, or a ring...'

'Gone,' I told him with a sigh.

He thought for a moment, then: 'Do they know you've no money at all?'

'The ones at the first gate do,' I answered. 'I don't know if the other does.'

'You mean the portly rogue outside?' And when I nodded:

'His name's Cotfield, and you'd best hope he doesn't learn of it too soon,' Curriter said. 'Once you've naught left, you're bound for The Hole... I expect you've heard tell of that pit.'

I swallowed; my mouth was parched again, but I would not beg Curriter for another drink. I had indeed heard of the notorious Hole, the last and worst place of confinement in the prison; yet until now, the prospect of ending up there had not even occurred to me. Aghast, I could only stare at him.

'What of your belt?' he asked on a sudden. 'The leather looks very fine.'

I followed his gaze – and hope stirred in my vitals. 'Do you think it would serve?' I asked. 'It cost me nine shillings - the buckle is good pewter.'

'Well, that's more than one of these varlets makes in a fortnight, aside from bribes,' Curriter said. 'If it were me, I would indeed try to trade; but you'll need all your wits about you to strike a bargain.'

'I see that,' I said, after a moment. 'And I thank heaven I met you in this god-forsaken house, sir – you have my undying gratitude.'

'You are right welcome, Robert,' was his reply. 'Despite our short acquaintance, it's been a pleasure.' He favoured me with a smile. 'As I said, I hope to be gone soon after mid-day. Now, if I were in your place, I would take some time to plan your strategy.' To which I could only nod, and wish him well.

And yet it was well into the afternoon before I could put my plan, such as it was, into practice.

During the day some of my fellows - the luckier ones - had been allowed out to take dinner elsewhere; like me, the rest remained unfed. I soon learned that the turnkeys never ventured beyond the doorway, usually when a new inmate was thrust inside to join us, as one was around mid-day: a poor, staggering fellow who from the look of him had been badly beaten. He arrived shortly after I'd said farewell to Curriter, who took his leave with good humour, though obvious relief. That a man could get himself sent here by design still struck me as unfathomable, unless perhaps he was in fear of his life as Curriter claimed - and had the means to bring his confinement to an end.

After he was gone I felt more alone than I'd done in years, and was in danger of falling into abject misery when I thought of those I loved and missed: Anne and Kate, Hester and Childers, the servants at Thirldon... even George. On one matter I was clear, however: Anne and George must not hear of my imprisonment. Anne would be in despair, while George would be outraged, fearing the disgrace it could bring upon his family, not to say his station. In truth, I do not believe he would have let me remain in the Counter, but would have found ways to get me released; yet I was resolved. Hence, I racked my brains to think who might help me in settling the debt I was accused of owing, by way of a loan I would, of course, repay. And in that matter, I began to have serious doubts.

For there were old friends, but they were few, with my having been absent from London for so long. Still seated in my dimly-lit corner, knees drawn up and wearing the hardest expression I could muster to keep intruders at bay, I began to count names, and found there were only three or four whose whereabouts I knew. And from those, I ended up with just one name: John Druett, the man Anne had spoken of at Highgate a mere three days earlier, though it now seemed long ago. Druett was a firm friend, a kindly if bluff man, and one not lacking in courage. On learning of the wrong done to me he would surely come to my aid, I thought; beyond that, I had little left to support my hopes.

Hence, to my strategy: the belt which whoever robbed me had been generous enough to leave behind. It was as Curriter had said: of good ox-hide, well-crafted and tooled, with a strong square buckle, though the hanger for my rapier had been taken off it along with the weapon. Nevertheless, I would puff up its value as I would do my best to win over the swag-bellied Cotfield. Having readied myself, I awaited an opportunity, but it was slow in coming. I was thinking of going to the door and banging upon it, demanding to speak to the turnkey on a matter of urgency, when it opened abruptly to admit a new prisoner. Stiffly I got to my feet, then made what haste I could before it was closed again.

'Master Cotfield.' Brushing past the new arrival, I seized the edge of the door. 'Will you hear me?'

The face of the man in question appeared, wearing an angry frown. And all he said was: 'Get your fucking hand away, or I'll spike it.'

'I want to do business,' I said. 'And I can pay handsomely.'

'You?' The man sneered. 'You haven't a farthing – don't try and cog me.'

'I speak not of coinage,' I said quickly. 'I mean this... will you look?' Before he could answer I proffered the belt which I had already removed, and laid it flat across my palms. I had earlier rubbed it with spittle, cleaned the buckle and buffed it to the best shine I could. At sight of it Cotfield hesitated, which was enough.

'It's of the best leather, fine-tooled,' I said, sounding like a street vendor. 'You see the quality - you can sell it for ten shillings. And it's yours if you'll take me out, to the house of a man who'll settle my debt. It's not far – Coleman Street. Now, what do you say?'

His reply, however, came as a disappointment.

'Sweet Jesus, I'd not take you anywhere,' he said in a voice of contempt. 'Not for a gold sovereign - someone's been playing you for a fool.'

'Then, will you deliver a message?' I asked, breathing fast. 'To the same man - John Druett, a lawyer in Coleman Street, close by the Armourer's Hall. He'll pay you – and the belt is yours, when I'm freed.'

At that, the man's frown eased somewhat. Looking down, he eyed my precious belt, scratching under his beard as if debating with himself. Finally he said:

'The belt, and your shoes, and I'll go to your lawyer friend first thing in the morning.'

'No!' In dismay, I shook my head. 'I cannot stay here another night. I meant you should go this evening.'

'But I won't,' came the reply. 'I'm not relieved for another hour, then I'm for home.' A crooked smile appeared. 'Home to a good supper and a warm bed, beside a nice warm body. What do *you* say?'

'Very well,' I said, my spirits sinking. 'In the morning, as soon as you can....' Then, as his words struck home: 'Wait -

surely you don't mean to leave me without my shoes? That would be intolerable.'

'Your belt and your shoes,' Cotfield threw back. 'And I promise nothing – I'll go, or perhaps I won't go. You'd best pray I'm in a good humour tomorrow. Now step away, before I throw you to the floor.'

I began to protest anew, but it was no use. A poniard appeared and was thrust under my nose whereupon, having no other choice, I yielded. 'The belt and shoes then,' I said, feeling the last shreds of my dignity fall away. 'I'll be waiting in the morning...' Since the door was already closing, I was obliged to lean round it and call through the gap. 'John Druett in Coleman Street – his old friend Belstrang begs his aid...'

There followed a thud, and the scrape of the heavy bolt being drawn across.

Whereupon Robert Belstrang was obliged to spend his second night in The Compter, in an even more miserable condition than on the first; for to have hopes raised which are slender as a thread, can be worse than having no hopes at all.

And yet for all that, the morning came, and I tasted freedom: the sweetest taste a man can savour, for which I have given thanks ever since.

TEN

He was waiting outside the gates in a drizzle, hatted and cloaked, legs planted apart as was his old habit, one gloved hand resting on his sword-hilt. He had never been a man who was easily surprised, but at sight of me when I emerged hungry, shoeless, bedraggled and filled with shame, his eyes widened.

'By all that's holy, Belstrang... what in God's name has become of you?'

I made no reply; I could have kissed him as if he were a brother, but I merely shook my head.

'Your feet...' He looked down, as I made my way towards him over the cobbles in my stockings. 'This is cruel usage indeed.'

'But it's over,' I said, attempting a smile. 'Thanks to you, in your goodness...' I put out my hand. 'I'm in your debt, John Druett, in more ways than you know.'

'I'm curious to hear about it,' he said as we shook hands. 'But that can wait; will you come to my house, where my servants will attend you?'

'Most gladly,' I answered. 'If you're not too troubled by my slowness of pace.' I indicated my stockings, filthy from my walk through the prison and now soaking wet. 'Perhaps we might find a fripperer's stall, and buy a cheap pair of shoes...'

'I'll not hear of such,' Druett said at once. 'My horse is nearby – you'll ride, and I'll walk beside you.' He indicated the grim frontage of the Compter. 'Let's get ourselves away from here.'

Which we did; and despite the cold rain that fell, it was a most welcome ride on Druett's good roan horse. Within the half hour we had made our way by Lad Lane and Catte Street, past Basinghall to crowded Lothbury and then into Coleman Street, to his house near the Armourers' Hall. Here, still weak from my brief ordeal, I was brought indoors and made welcome by Frances Druett; at sight of her, I almost sagged with relief.

'Robert...?' Her smile fading, she looked me up and down. 'What's this – have you been robbed?'

'I have, dear Frances,' I answered, 'yet of nothing that can't be replaced. As for my pride, and a good deal of my trust: those, I fear, will not be so easily restored.'

Whereupon, seeing her come forward to embrace me, I confess I wept a little. That is how low I'd been brought: to fall like a milksop on to a woman's shoulder, and stain her gown with my tears.

Still, it was a blessed day, which lifted my spirits greatly. It was as though years fell away, in the company of people who had been among my closest friends, and who were eager to succour me. In a short time I was given a chamber with a good bed, water and soap to wash, hose and a fresh shirt loaned by Druett. After hearing the barest summary of my plight, he ordered two of his servants to go to the Bel Savage, retrieve my belongings from my chamber and bring Leucippus from the stable. When I spoke of the reckoning, he dismissed the matter: his men would settle what was owed, and I could repay him when I was ready. I was now his guest for as long as I chose; he was deaf to any other suggestion. When I had taken a little food and drink I should rest for the afternoon, after which my host and his wife expected me to join them at supper. Hence, by the time I had taken this in, my faith in human kindness was greatly replenished, even if I almost swayed where I stood for lack of rest. Thereafter I slept like a babe, waking when night had fallen and a servant came with a candle to light me downstairs. In his other hand was a pair of shoes, loose-buckled; the master was of a longer foot than mine, the man said, but these should serve me until the morrow.

Sitting on the bed, I thanked him as if he too were one of my rescuers; which in a manner, he was.

It was a most memorable supper, which owed little to the food, good though that was. Sated, restored in body and spirit with a cup of sweet wine before me, I could only thank my hosts profusely. For, despite the grim predictions of those rascally turnkeys in the Compter, my belongings had been found at the Bel Savage and brought away safely. More importantly,

Leucippus was now housed in Druett's stable at the rear of the house, watered and fed. When I enquired after the ostler, whom I no longer trusted to tell me the time of day, I learned that the man was absent. So, leaving him aside, I told my entire story to the Druetts over supper, from first arriving in London to the present. By the time it was done, and we sat with empty plates before us, both of them were amazed; perhaps it was as much their Year of Astonishment as it was mine.

'By all the saints,' Druett said at last. 'You've walked into a firestorm.'

'So it would seem,' I said.

'And here's another puzzle: though I paid your debt of twenty-five pounds, I'm in ignorance of whom the recipient is.' And when I asked how that could be:

'The warrant was made out by a third party – a lawyer named Darby, whose client wishes to withhold his name. Knowing what I do of Darby, it would be no use asking him: he's as tight-mouthed as an eel – and tight-fisted, too.'

'Well then, it's all of a piece,' I said, after digesting the news. 'For I've been kept in ignorance of a good many things over the past week – in truth, ever since I went to Bedlam and sought out poor Thomas Jessop.'

'From what you've told, that does appear to have angered someone,' Druett said. 'Someone who wants you gone, and is prepared to use any means to force you – even to seeing you perish in prison. It would have looked as though you'd died of sickness – somewhat conveniently perhaps, for someone?'

'For Edmund Anstis,' I said, after a moment. 'You'll know him, I think - it was he who warned me off.'

'Indeed, I do know him,' Druett said, with a glance at his wife. 'Most friendly nowadays with the new favourite Villiers. Anstis was all but unknown two years back, when he was little better than a clerk at the embassy in the Hague - now he's everywhere. He serves Sir Thomas Lake, the joint Secretary.'

'Does he?' I found myself frowning. 'Odd that he chose not to speak of that when we dined together. I'd have thought it something to boast about.'

Druett was silent, pondering the matter. Turning to Frances, I murmured an apology for the turn the conversation had taken, to which she gave a sigh.

'I no longer interest myself in matters of state, Robert,' she said. 'This is not the England we knew when we were young, is it? Not that Elizabeth's last years were good times, but we always believed she cared for her people - unlike our King, who fears the crowd and scorns anyone who doesn't admire him. He's called no parliament for two years, because they won't allow him more money – and now we learn of scandals aplenty, courtiers accused of poisoning their enemies in the Italian fashion... I envy you your distance from it, away in the country.'

'In truth, that's what Anstis told me,' I said with a wry smile. 'That I should give up my business here, and go back home.'

I looked to John Druett. 'Yet, I'm even less inclined to do that now. I heartily dislike being treated as I have been. You might recall my obduracy...'

'When we were at Gray's Inn together? I do, as if it were yesterday,' Druett broke in. 'As I recall the troubles you brought upon yourself by it.' He gave a smile, as old friends do when common memories spring up, whereupon Frances chose her moment to rise from the table.

'I'll leave you to talk of such things,' she said. 'And it seems there's a good deal else to be turned and turned about, as John would put it.' As she left the table, she placed a hand on her husband's shoulder. 'Though you'll find a remedy in the end – you always do.'

After she was gone, we indeed began to ponder the matter into which I had blundered a week ago - beginning with Thomas Jessop, and his supposed plot to assassinate the King, as was done to Henri of France. Whereupon, Druett lost no time in giving me his opinion.

'It's preposterous,' he said flatly. 'Madmen may prate of such, but no sane man would even contemplate it. Nobody forgets the Powder Treason. The King is protected at all times, and no stranger is allowed near.'

'No sane man,' I replied. 'But a fanatic who has lost all reason, like the assassin Ravaillac.'

'And yet your friend Jessop had enough reason left to abandon the scheme, if he ever dreamed it up at all,' Druett countered. 'Which might account for his losing his wits, and ending up in Bedlam.'

'Perhaps,' I allowed. 'But when he was raving in the street, he cried out he'd been a dupe and a gull, which suggests to me he'd been used by others. There's also the matter of the money he had, to pay for sword lessons among other things, the source of which is a mystery. And more – what of the armed men who came for him at the house of Jane Rudlin, terrifying her with their threats? There are simply too many factors to dismiss – I've had ample time to think on them, while mewed up in that foul prison.'

'Very well, my friend…' Druett drew breath. 'Let's say I've donned my lawyer's gown, and am ready to hear your argument. The accused is a madman, unfit to plead his case, so it falls to you to speak of him. Will you proceed?'

'I will,' I said, fortifying myself with a gulp of wine. '*In primis*, let us suppose that this troubled young man, a devout proponent of his faith, truly intended to carry out the heinous crime of regicide, in emulation of the plotters of ten years before, and on the anniversary of their attempt. After all, there have been rumours enough since then of new Popish Plots, and accusations flung at those who are despised for their religion - even men of high rank.'

Wearing his advocate's face, Druett watched me.

'*Secundus*,' I continued, 'the youth gets himself to London, where he manages to find a priest, who sends him to Papists to seek lodging. Perhaps the priest gives him a little money, but surely not enough to live as he did: taking lessons in swordsmanship, drinking freely and paying promptly for his board. Thomas then writes to his father, and in what sounds like his last letter he speaks of making his family proud, of giving succour to others – and of striking a blow for all those he termed "of our benighted faith". Moreover, he lets slip to Mistress Rudlin that he has some grand purpose in mind – even to being the English Ravaillac. Do you mark all that?'

'And *tertius*?' Druett said, his face blank.

'*Tertius*, Jessop is indiscreet – too much of a hothead to keep his plans a close secret. And quite soon, perhaps from a priest, who has likely been questioned at some point, someone else hears of this young zealot: someone with the will to encourage him in his plan, and the means to pay him – in short, to set him on as the regicide, while himself remaining hidden. For such a man, or even a group of such, would that not be an opportunity to be seized and cherished?'

'It might,' was Druett's reply. 'But the risk would still be great: if Jessop's loose-tongued as you say, he would succumb to questioning, and name his accomplices.'

'Who would likely have foreseen such a danger, and got themselves elsewhere,' I countered. 'As the plotters did in 1605, leaving Fawkes to bear the risk.'

'They left London to raise an insurrection, counting on the Parliament being blown up and the King being dead,' Druett objected. 'So far as I'm aware, there have been no rumours of men, horses or weaponry being amassed anywhere, let alone of Papists being particularly active. Most are cowed and broken, like your neighbour John Jessop.'

I paused, mulling the matter over. Laying it out as I had done helped me to view it more clearly, to the extent that I questioned my own argument: could it truly have happened thus? Could young Thomas Jessop, in his raw passion, have been so rash – and so easily used? I saw again the face of his father, sitting in my parlour at Thirldon, and knew how his son's actions would, at the least, ruin him and his wife; and at the worst, send them to their deaths.

'But then again…' Druett interrupted my thoughts, placing his hands flat upon the table as he was wont to do. 'If such a treasonous plot were truly hatched, the right course would indeed be to uncover the perpetrators, even if their plans were never brought to fruition. Should you succeed in doing so, you could find yourself well rewarded – perhaps to the extent of a knighthood, without your having to buy one. The going rate is thirty pounds, I hear.'

'I've no such motive,' I said at once, taken aback by his thin smile. 'My concern is to piece out what happened to Thomas, get him released and see him restored to his family.'

'I know it - and in doing so, you run the same risks as before,' my host replied. 'You may be watched, now you've left the prison. If you intend to go about, you should hire a sturdy and well-armed man to accompany you.'

'I will,' I said, 'for I do indeed intend to go about.'

'Then I'll loan you the money you need, for as long as you need it,' Druett said, after a moment. 'You'll want a new sword, clothes and other stuffs.'

Moved by his words, I put out my hand and grasped his. 'Of all the names I thought of in the prison,' I said, 'yours was the only one I knew I could call upon, without condition. And yet I'll not draw you into this business, for I've no inkling where it might lead. I should find somewhere else to lodge-'

'There's no need,' came the prompt reply. 'I'm hosting an old friend, nothing more. Besides, I'm not without influence – I might even be of help. For one thing I'm acquainted with Jenner, the keeper of Bedlam, though I'd not want him as a friend. I'll make enquiry for you, as to who pays for Jessop's board.'

'Once again, you have my deepest thanks,' was all I could say. But in truth I was daunted again by the task which lay ahead: more so now, since the experience of being falsely imprisoned. Seeing my expression, Druett spoke up.

'I've yet to be convinced by your theory,' he said, 'but I'll admit that it troubles me. It might be best to think on who might be capable of such a desperate act, if anyone was – to seize the opportunity you spoke of. Those who hate King James enough to risk everything, in the hopes that their religion may yet be restored, as some think possible…'

'You mean, if the Spanish Match were to go ahead?' I broke in.

Druett was sceptical again. 'I cannot believe that will happen. But men will clutch at straws…' He frowned. 'And it's true there are many embittered Papists. The Countess of Shrewsbury comes to mind, only lately released from the Tower - a strong woman, who loathes the King.'

'What of the Earl of Northumberland?' I asked. 'Still

imprisoned in the Tower, yet rich enough to fund a whole regiment?'

'I don't believe he's a threat,' Druett replied. 'Dotty and deaf, content with his books and scientific experiments, while living in comfort.' Then, as a thought struck him: 'And yet, if some plot against the King were uncovered, such nobles would indeed be suspect.'

'As would all Papists of substance,' I added. 'And of course, the Spanish.'

'Oddly enough, I would discount the Spanish,' Druett said. 'That weasel of an ambassador, Sarmiento, has worked hard to get the King to approve the Match for the prince - as have crypto-Catholics on the Council. They'd never be party to any plot – they've too much to lose.'

'What of Sir Thomas Lake?' I said, recalling what George had told me. 'He's a Papist...' But Druett was shaking his head.

'Lake's an arse-kisser who cares only for his own advancement, and besides he hasn't the courage. If I discounted anyone, it would be him.'

'This is a maze,' I said, weary all of a sudden. 'It seems to make less sense, the more I look at it. For one thing, if some Papist - or more than one - had urged Thomas Jessop to such a wild course of action, why would Anstis tell me to keep my nose out? He may work for Lake as you say, but he's no Papist – far from it.'

'Only he can answer that question,' Druett said. 'He, or perhaps your Bedlamite. But then he's mad, or pretending to be...' he stifled a yawn. 'May we sleep on it? Tomorrow you may follow your trail, such as it is, while I go to my work. By supper-time, you may even have made progress.'

Then with a tired smile, he added: 'For if you've not lost faith in me, Justice Belstrang, nor have I in you.'

My hired man was named Oldrigg; and if he put fear into any man, he surely frightened me. On Druett's advice, I went to the Armourers' Hall the morning after our supper talk and was recommended to a fellow who lived not far away. He had been a soldier, of course, and was well suited to my purpose: which *in primis* was to go again to Richard Elms the fencing master, and question him further.

It was little more than a whim, but since I had few choices I believed it worth the attempt. Being well rested and breakfasted, and with a vigour I had all but lost in the Compter, I ventured out into the cloudy day and, with money lent by Druett, went swiftly about my business: purchasing shoes, a belt and a good rapier with hanger and scabbard. Then with Oldrigg at my heels, I left the city via Cripplegate and walked through St Giles to Aldersgate Street, to the house with the sign of crossed swords.

I was clearer-headed now, for my discourse with Druett had helped a good deal. First thing that morning I had sent further letters to Hester and to John Jessop, telling them that I was delayed and would write again. Then, pacing my chamber, I had ordered my thoughts. For the plain fact was that, unfashionable as it might seem in the thirteenth year of the reign of King James, I still believed in honour and in justice, and would uphold them as I had tried to do as a country magistrate. Thus resolved, I now entered the fencing hall, walked straight into the middle of the chalked circle and called aloud for Richard Elms.

There was an immediate silence from the several men who were present. Pausing at their swordplay and their conversation, they all turned to look - not at me but at Oldrigg, who stood like a challenger come to take on anyone who dared. The silence persisted as Elms himself appeared from the rear in his buff coat, making his way through the fencers – and at sight of me, his face clouded.

'I've naught else to say to you, sir,' he said at once. 'I told you all I knew last time…' his gaze wandered to Oldrigg, whereupon he stiffened. 'And what can you mean, bringing this man here?'

'He's a friend,' I answered. 'Is there somewhere more private, where we may converse?'

'There is not.' Having come as close as he would, Elms stood defiant. 'And I know nothing further of Philip Mayne, as I've said.'

'Then let me enlighten you,' I replied. 'Philip Mayne is

starving himself to death in a madhouse, in torment for some perceived wrong he committed. The swordsmanship he tried to learn from you may have some bearing on it – have you anything to say to that?'

I was bluffing, of course, and perhaps said more than I'd intended - but if I hoped to startle Elms, I was disappointed. This man had fought for his life, faced untold dangers and was unafraid - or so I concluded. I was about to try another question when I was diverted by Oldrigg, who bent close and spoke in my ear.

'Tell him Mayne was preparing to fight a duel,' he murmured. 'It's unlawful. He could face a fine if he's proven to be aiding duellists – as he's been known to do.'

Keeping expression from my face, I barely nodded; those may have been the first words Oldrigg had uttered since we walked from his lodgings, but they were most apposite. Drawing breath, I fixed Elms with a hard eye - and lied shamelessly.

'Perhaps I should have added that I spoke at length with Master Mayne,' I stated. 'It seems he had challenged an important man to a duel, and was determined to see it through despite his lack of skill with a sword. Given the King's strong disapproval of duelling, they planned to go out to a remote place and fight – and you, his teacher, would stand as Mayne's second. That's what he told me.'

Wearing my blandest look, I waited. At first the words seemed to have no effect – then came a burst of righteous anger.

'By the Christ, that's a whoreson lie!' Elms exclaimed. 'I never heard any such intent from Mayne, nor would I have aided him. I'm a loyal subject, who obeys the law!'

'Do you, always?' I said, savouring my advantage. 'It's not what I've heard. Then, who would blame a man - especially if the duellist offers enough money.'

'Lies!' Elms repeated, though he looked flushed now. 'And I won't have anyone coming here with accusations...' He broke off, frowning, and looked round at his customers who were very still, every man hanging on his words. When he turned back to me, I put on a smile and gestured to the doorway.

'Can we not go outside to talk?' I asked. 'I think the rain's holding off.'

ELEVEN

We stood in the bustle of Aldersgate Street, close to the wall to avoid the carts that passed from time to time. Elms was still angry, and wary of Oldrigg who would likely have been his match, and both men knew it. He continued to insist that he knew nothing of any duel his pupil Mayne intended, which of course was true. And yet, seeing his unease, a notion struck me.

'Has anyone else come to talk to you about Mayne?' I asked, observing him closely. 'Since I was here?'

Elms replied that they had not.

'The matter is,' I went on, stretching my tale, 'that the one Mayne took offence at, in his rashness, is a nobleman well-known to the King. If His Majesty got to hear that you were teaching this man's challenger, he'd be most displeased – would he not?' I asked this of Oldrigg, who nodded.

'Likely he'd close Master Elms down,' he said gently.

'So, I'd counsel you to talk to me,' I said to Elms, 'before I talk to someone important.' And when he gave no answer: 'Who was it, who came to warn you to keep your mouth tight-shut?'

Another pause followed, while Elms weighed his choices. Then, with a glance at Oldrigg, he faced me and said: 'Will you give me your word as a gentleman, that you'll leave my name out of this?'

'That depends on what you tell me,' I answered.

'I want your word. Or I go back inside now, and you can do as you please.'

'Very well…' after appearing to ponder the matter, I nodded – and decided to go on the attack. 'First, tell me this: are you acquainted with a man named Edmund Anstis?' To which, Elms's response took me by surprise.

'Good Christ - if you already know that, then why do you press me?' He demanded. 'Do you play some cat-and-mouse game?'

'I do not,' I answered. 'And I'd like to hear what you know of the man.'

'Well, it's no more than others do,' came the terse reply. 'He used to come here a year or two back, after he returned from the Low Countries. He served the ambassador, in The Hague. After the Truce he stayed on, like I did.' He hesitated, then: 'Yet, unlike me, he was too fond of cards and tables - got himself into debt. He was loth to come home penniless, so he turned watchman in Flushing: skulking about the wharfs, ferreting out pieces of intelligence for Lord Cecil.'

'And when Lord Cecil died?' I prompted.

'What do you think?' Elms retorted. 'Anstis was left masterless and unpaid, as were others. He got himself back to England somehow, and that's all I know.'

He was impatient to be gone, for which I could hardly censor him; but he could not know he had set my mind racing about Anstis. I made as if I was ready to leave, then aimed another question.

'You must have some inkling of what Anstis did after he came home. He was a customer, and you had Dutch service in common... will you throw me a scrap? My word still holds.'

'By the...' Elms cursed under his breath. 'Will you not rest, until you've got me hanging by my thumbs?'

I waited; beside me, Oldrigg made a low rumble in his throat.

'He was an informer on Papists.' Elms almost spat the words out. 'He infiltrated secret masses, winkled priests out of their holes – one of those beneficiaries of recusancy, at up to fifty pounds reward. For all I know, he may be still - and though he was my customer, I say the man's a cur. Now, is that enough for you?'

I made no reply, for in truth I was confounded. That Anstis, a prosperous lawyer who served men of high rank, should have occupied such a trade as informing on Catholic families for reward... at thought of it, he sank even lower in my estimation. But I was stirred and excited, for I knew I'd heard something of value to use against the man who, I felt certain, was responsible for getting me imprisoned. Drawing a breath, I nodded at Elms, who lost no time turning on his heel and walking back inside his fencing school. As he went he threw me a baleful look, that carried warning enough: I would be ill-advised to come here again.

Oldrigg and I walked in silence along Aldersgate Street, until my hired man drew alongside me, and made a confession that stopped me in my tracks.

'Perhaps I should have told you, sir: I'm of the Roman faith myself.'

And when I turned to him: 'I too fought in the Dutch war – but on the other side. In the English Regiment, under Stanley: that rabble of renegades, as folk call us. I was younger back then, and fired up... now I follow the King's laws. But if you wish me to quit your service, I would understand.'

'Well... just now, I need a mug of something strong while I ponder my next step,' I told him, after taking a breath. 'Yet if you'd prefer to quit my service rather than drink with a man who once levied fines upon Catholics, I too would understand.'

'However,' I added, as the burly ex-soldier met my gaze, 'if you'd care to accompany me while I seek those with whom I have bones to pick, I'd be willing enough to have you at my side.'

To which, the briefest of nods was all the answer I required. And though a short time earlier I might have berated myself for hiring a man who had fought against the Crown's allies, which made him a traitor, I viewed him for the plain fellow he was; perhaps I even liked him. Or, perhaps I was so jubilant with uncovering those pieces of Anstis's past – levers with which to prise the truth out of him – that just then I would have supped with the Pope himself.

For how many Catholic families, I wondered, would like to know who informed on them for having mass said in their homes, let alone for harbouring priests? How many wives could speak of husbands thrown into prison – of some who had even taken their lives in despair? How many children could tell of fathers ruined, of inheritances lost? Thomas Jessop could, for one; and at thought of him my mood darkened. How, I asked myself, could he and a man like Edmund Anstis be linked – and why in heaven's name would they be?

I see now, that I had only scratched the surface of the anthill.

The afternoon was fair, with a strong wind sending the clouds off to the east. Oldrigg and I emerged from the ordinary where we had fed our appetites, and made our way to Ludgate. I had decided that Anstis could wait a while, until I had been back to the Bel Savage and questioned people: that rogue of an ostler for one, and the drawer who had filled my cup for Mary Wedd. I bore a powerful resentment towards anyone who might have been a part of having me imprisoned.

Arriving at the inn, we walked into the yard and made directly for the stables. And there was my man, the shameless bawd who had offered to procure a trull for my bed. At sight of me, he appeared taken aback.

'Well now...' Hand on sword, I strode towards him. 'What, did you not expect to see me again?'

'I did not, sir.' His eyes went swiftly to Oldrigg, and back to me. 'I thought you were gone, seeing as Leucippus was taken away.'

'Gone from London? Or gone somewhere else?'

'In truth, master, I had no notion...' the man wet his lips nervously. 'So, how can I aid you today?'

'You can tell me about Mary Wedd,' I answered, watching his reaction.

'Who?' A puzzled look appeared. 'I know nobody of that name.'

'Indeed?' I put on a puzzled look of my own. 'You, who offered to supply a woman of the best quality, to suit my tastes? I urge you to think again.'

'I've no need to,' came the reply. 'For I swear the name is unknown to me.'

'Red taffeta gown, copper-coloured periwig, and a very tempting smile,' I said. 'Three days ago, soon after you and I spoke on this very spot, she accosted me in the inn. Do you mean to say you didn't send her?'

'In God's name, I do say so.' He screwed his eyes up in that manner he had. 'And as for the picture you've just made, it might be true of any whore in London.'

I looked closely at him, thinking that if he was spinning me a yarn, he was a most accomplished liar. I glanced at Oldrigg, who was eying the man without expression.

'If you didn't send her to me, who else could have?' I demanded. And when no reply was forthcoming I took a step forward, startling him.

'Peace, sir... there's no need,' he said. 'You were a customer who paid well – my only wish was to serve you, as I've served many a gentleman who lacks company at night. And I wouldn't have sent a woman to you, after you refused. Moreover, I would have bespoke one to come to your chamber at night, or to meet you for a tryst elsewhere. Master Tucker doesn't like it otherwise.'

'Tucker...' I recalled the name of one of the inn servants - the one who had told me of Anstis's arrival. 'You collude with him in your whoring trade, do you?'

'I'd not put it so, master.' The ostler swallowed noisily. 'Only, if you mean to go to him, I'd be most obliged if you'd not speak of this... that is...what's passed between us, I mean.'

'We'll see, shall we?' I raised a hand and pointed, causing the fellow to flinch. 'For if I'm dissatisfied with what I hear, I'll return very soon.'

I turned about and, with Oldrigg following, went directly to the main room of the inn. The place was busy, crammed with afternoon drinkers and tobacco takers. Moving to the rear where the barrels were stacked, I found Tucker himself working the spigot, while drawers hurried back and forth with mugs in hand. As I approached, the man looked up.

'You'll remember me,' I said. 'I was last here three days ago, drinking your best sack. Only, the last cup quickly sent me to sleep. Odd, wouldn't you say?'

Unlike the ostler, however, Tucker was not a man to be cowed easily. With barely a glance at Oldrigg, who stood by with arms folded, he continued to fill a mug with frothy beer.

'In truth, sir, we're so busy that I forget who was here by the end of each day, let alone three days back,' he said. 'And yet, if you've a complaint about the sack, I'll gladly pour you a cup free of the charge, and a mug for your servant here. Find a place, and I'll send a boy over.'

'I will not,' I replied. 'Nor will I leave, until you tell me about

Mary Wedd.'

There was no reaction, save a lifting of the man's eyebrows. 'Who?'

'I think you know who I mean,' I countered, reining in my impatience. 'She brought my cup to be refilled – only when it came to me, there was more than sack in it. I was drugged, then robbed and ill-used - and I mean to have redress. I'm speaking of the law against procurement, at the least. The penalty for poisoning, however, is somewhat more severe.'

Tucker stepped away, handed a filled mug to a potboy, then beckoned to another drawer. When the man came he told him to work the spigot, then spoke quietly.

'We'd best talk out here, sir,' he said, and led the way. Once we were outside in a narrow, dim-lit passageway, however, his demeanour changed markedly.

'You've no call to threaten me,' he said. 'I but do the landlord's bidding: serve food and drink, and pass the time of day with customers. As for the woman you speak of, I know her by reputation only-'

'She's a trull for hire, who would make me her customer,' I broke in. 'And I don't believe she could have put something in my cup without you seeing it.'

But when he shook his head firmly, I tensed: I had encountered his sort often, who would deny everything unto their last breath. It was time for Oldrigg to earn his wage, I thought - and on that, he needed no prompting. To Tucker's alarm my guard thrust out a hand, clasped the man about the neck and began to squeeze.

'Enough of your dissembling,' he growled, pushing his face close to the other's. 'My master will have answers, or we'll haul you off to a magistrate. You'll not be passing the time of day with anyone then, except your fellow prisoners.'

'By Christ…' the man's hands flew up to seize Oldrigg's arm, then felt his assailant's superior strength. 'Leave me be… I'm not the one…'

'Mary Wedd.' I snapped the name out. 'What's she to you?'

'She's nothing to me…' he grunted as Oldrigg tightened his grip, and stared about, but there was no-one in sight. 'For pity's sake - a whore's a whore, as common as fleas. I neither know nor care who she plies her trade with…'

'She brought my cup to be filled, and put something in it,' I repeated. 'That's not how whores ply their trade, is it? Unless they've been instructed by someone else – so, was it you who supplied the potion?'

'Jesus, no!' The man spat. 'I would never…'

He was growing red in the face, sweat beading his brow. But when he struggled harder against Oldrigg, my man pushed him against the wall. 'Speak up, friend,' he muttered. 'I can keep this up for a half hour, if need be.'

'Enough!' Tucker made a choking sound, and his eyes went to Oldrigg's. ''Will you squeeze the life from me?' he gulped. 'How would that serve you?'

'Tell me what I want to know,' I said. 'And point me to where I can find Mary Wedd. And if I'm satisfied, we're finished here.'

'By the Christ…' In anger and shame, our captive muttered an oath; but his unwillingness to talk had already convinced me of his involvement. Before I could press him further he removed a hand from Oldrigg's arm and flapped it in submission. Whereupon, at a nod from me, my man released him.

'I only do as I'm told,' he panted, throwing a baleful look at his tormentor. 'Nor do I ask questions. A man comes to me and says what must happen, pays me to do my part, then tells me never to speak of it. More, he knows I have a son, and where he and his mother dwell - I swear, I'd no choice but to obey!'

'And what was your part?' I asked.

He hesitated, rubbing his chafed neck, then: 'I was to await the right moment, then tell Mary Wedd where you were; she was nearby, and would come in quickly. She'd beg the price of a mug from you, then serve it herself. After I'd poured, I was to look away as she took it, so I saw nothing. But once you were senseless I had to get you out to the street, as if you were soused. There, a sergeant-at-mace was waiting to serve a warrant on you - I know not what for. I left you with him and his deputy, then went inside. And that was the end of my part – I swear it.'

I took in his statement, and believed that it tallied well enough with what had followed. So: a sergeant-at mace had delivered me to the Compter by due process; perhaps even he was ignorant that the charge was false. And likely there was no need to seek out Mary Wedd now, who had merely been paid to do her part as had Tucker. The setter-on, of course, was the one to seek... and a single name came to mind.

'That day, when you stopped me by the stairs and told me a gentleman was asking for me.' I fixed my eye on Tucker. 'You claimed not to know him - was that true?'

After a moment, the man shook his head.

'Was it he who paid you to summon Mary Wedd, and help her do his bidding?' I demanded. And when his silence was answer enough: 'Have you served this man before? Answer me - or I'll have you clapped up for an attempt at poisoning.'

'I've not, I swear, only...' he lowered his gaze. 'When he came to me that day you rode off, I told him you were lodging here; though in truth, he seemed to have guessed it already.'

'And do you know who that man is, and whom he serves?'

'His name's Anstis,' came the answer, at last. 'But as for who he serves, I do not...' he threw a bitter look at Oldrigg. 'And you can rack me till doomsday, for there's naught else I can tell! Now can I go, or do you mean to lose me my place?'

'I wouldn't want that,' I replied. 'Since, as long as you work here, I'll know where to find you.' And I turned to Oldrigg who, at a nod, followed me outside.

We did not speak for some time, my hired man walking beside me through Ludgate, by St Paul's and then down towards the river, crossing Thames Street until we stood at Paul's Stairs where I hailed a wherry. As it drew near, the waterman plashing oars in his haste to claim a passenger, Oldrigg asked where we were bound, and was uneasy with my answer.

'Whitehall? I'd not expected that, Master Robert.'

'Well, it's of no great matter,' I said. I thought I understood: he was wary of being seen by guards who might be suspicious of him – who might even have known him, and what he once was. In my eagerness I had forgotten – but in my eagerness, I was in no humour to delay.

'I could dismiss you for the remainder of the day,' I said, watching the boatman draw up at the jetty. 'But let me offer you a choice: we part here, and I'll pay you – or you can accompany me to the Palace, and wait outside while I conduct my business. Which is to put the fear of God into Edmund Anstis who, as you heard from our friend master Elms, caused misery and mayhem to many of your faith – and may well have sent me to what he thought was my death. So, will you come with me or no?'

To my satisfaction, Oldrigg's answer was a grim smile; and without further word we clambered into the boat.

TWELVE

It was a short if chilly journey upon the water, against both wind and tide, the boatman straining at his oars. We passed the fine houses of noblemen, their gardens reaching from the Strand down to the river's edge, then turned up the great bend of the Thames, with Lambeth Palace visible on the far bank. Now Whitehall was close: the vast, ramshackle collection of buildings that had been knocked about and added to so often, a visitor was lost soon after he ventured inside. We docked at Whitehall Stairs, where I paid our fare while Oldrigg got ashore and put out a hand to steady me. Then it was but a short walk to the Court Gate, where I took my leave of him.

'I'm not sure how long I shall be,' I told him. 'But if it's longer than an hour, you may go where you will.' Reaching for my purse, I was counting out coins when a notion flew to mind: in my haste I had forgotten to enquire at the Bel Savage whether there was word from John Jessop, who would likely have answered my first letter to that address. Hence, for better or worse I decided to proceed without protection, and bade Oldrigg return to the inn, which relieved him somewhat. If there was a letter, he should bring it to Druett's house in Coleman Street.

We parted and I entered the palace, walking passages I had not trod in many years. As always, the place was abuzz with people, from servants in livery to courtiers in garish clothes, even a lord with men about him, richly attired. I knew my way to Westminster Hall, the common place of business for lawyers, where I might with luck find Edmund Anstis. Luck, however, was lacking, for on enquiry I learned that the King was away hunting at Royston. The Presence Chamber was all but empty, I was told - so if I had come here to petition, it was of no use.

I paused in a corridor to collect my thoughts. For if the King was away with his favoured 'hunting crew', as they were called, it was almost certain that Sir Thomas Lake was gone with him, and perhaps Anstis too. Disappointed by the thought of my journey being wasted, I decided nevertheless to go on to the Hall where I might get word of my quarry. On turning a corner, however, I found the way blocked by a cluster of people. Almost at once guards with halberds arrived to clear a path, whereupon we were all obliged to stand aside; clearly someone of great importance was about to pass. To my irritation I was ushered to the wall beside a perfumed gallant in a cream doublet shot with silver, who regarded my plain attire with distaste. But on a sudden, I was distracted by hearing someone mutter the words 'His Grace the Duke'.

'Pardon me, sir…' I addressed the dandy. 'Is it the Prince who is coming by?'

The man put on a pained look. 'Well sir, I know of no other Duke who resides in the Palace save the Duke of York, who is also the Prince – do you?'

Nettled by his insolence, I might have replied, but there was a stir among the watchers, and hats were quickly removed. I took off my own, just as a body of men in royal livery appeared. Thereafter, in spite of myself I was as intrigued as everyone else, as silence fell and men bowed their heads.

In the midst of several attendants and armed guards walked a slight, pale youth swathed in a voluminous suit of clothes: elaborate ruff, gold-threaded doublet with a red silk cloak over the shoulder, wide Spanish breeches and crimson knee-stocks, the whole affair garnished with silken ribbons; even the shoes were almost hidden under huge rosettes. There was just time to take in the spectacle before I was obliged to make my bow, while the Prince Charles walked past, seemingly indifferent to anyone's presence but his own.

This, then, since the death of his older brother, was the heir to the throne, whom I had never seen before: a boy of fifteen years, delicate in appearance and, if rumour were to be believed, somewhat dull-witted. Pressed by the onlookers, I watched as the group moved away, and was surprised by my perfumed neighbour who was busy replacing his bejewelled hat.

'To think we could see him married to a chit of a Spaniard,' the man muttered, seemingly unconcerned whether I heard or not. 'May God keep us from it.'

I stood as the watchers dispersed, the dandy among them. By

sheer chance I had been presented with the living prospect of the Spanish Match, which divided the Council and which, here at Whitehall, was a real danger to some. Just then, aside from the fall of the last royal favourite, it seemed people talked of little else. My discourse with Druett, and my earlier one with George, came quickly to mind: of the King's apparent willingness to see his son and heir betrothed to the Infanta, Maria Anna. Thinking hard upon it, I began moving again, finally emerging from a doorway into King Street.

Walking in the strong wind I gathered myself, and proceeded through a gateway into New Palace Yard, where I stopped beside the fountain. Facing me was Westminster Hall, from the doors of which a black-gowned lawyer was emerging, with a harassed-looking servant at his heels clutching papers. But on making brief enquiry of them, my spirits lifted: Edmund Anstis, secretary to Master Secretary Lake, had a room nearby, I was told; and more, the man was at his work today.

For a while I stood, drawing strong breaths of rather noisome riverside air; then I ventured inside, found the door and knocked hard upon it.

It was opened by a clerk in dusty black, who was surprised at sight of a stranger. Blocking the entry, the man took in my station quickly; but on asking my business, he was unsatisfied with the answer: that it was for the ears of Master Anstis only.

'He is most busy, sir,' the man said. 'However, if you wish to submit a petition for Secretary Lake when he returns from the country, I'll convey it to my master.'

'I don't,' I told him. 'I'll speak with Anstis, and no-one else.'

'As I said, sir,' came the swift reply, 'that isn't possible.'

'I think it is,' I said. And to the man's displeasure I pushed the door half-open, to reveal a well-lit chamber and chests piled with documents. 'Anstis!' I called. 'It's Belstrang, fresh from the Compter. May I come in, or shall I wait outside?'

A moment passed in which I heard movement from within, and what sounded like a muffled oath. The clerk, unsure of his ground, turned away to address his master, whereupon I took the opportunity to thrust myself between him and the door. And there was Anstis, on his feet behind a cluttered writing table, looking at me with mingled annoyance and embarrassment.

Neither of us spoke. At first, from the man's demeanour, it occurred to me that he would call for men-at-arms and have me ejected. But on seeing the humour I was in, he was more unsettled than I expected. Of course, I reasoned, since the false debt had been paid off, he must have known that I'd been freed from the prison; yet I doubt it had occurred to him that I would confront him in this way. And when he hesitated, I seized the advantage.

'You might wish to dismiss your servant,' I said, indicating his clerk. 'Or perhaps we could walk outside, by the fountain. It was always a favourite spot of mine.'

He met my gaze, but did not reply. The clerk, discomforted by the sudden tension in the room, gave a discreet cough and asked his master if he would prefer to have private discourse with the gentleman.

'That would be best,' I said, whereupon Anstis gave a sigh of exasperation and nodded. Once we were alone, however, he quickly gave vent to his anger.

'You walk on thin ice, Belstrang,' he said harshly, eying the door which was slightly ajar. 'How dare you come to me in this manner?'

'Why, what will you do?' I countered. 'Swear out another warrant against me, for a debt that never existed? I know how you got me into prison - and it's I who have grounds for having you arrested. I doubt you'd find the Compter to your taste, as I can testify from first-hand knowledge.'

'In God's name, what is it you want?' was his angry reply. 'I've no time to stand here in fruitless debate-'

'There's also the matter of the theft of my money, as well as my rapier and dagger,' I persisted. 'Which given their value, amounts to a serious felony.'

'I said, what do you want?' Anstis snapped.

'I'd like some answers. Though I've already learned a great deal these past few days – some of it about you.'

'Indeed?' He tried to assume his advocate's face. 'I hope it was entertaining.'

'Intriguing, is how I'd put it. Much of it concerns Thomas

Jessop, of whom you warned me to keep clear. Now that I know what that young man was planning to do, I cannot help but think of those who aided him – and why they did so.'

It was rash of me, I see now; and to this day I am unsure whether I meant to throw out veiled accusations. But to my surprise I saw that I was gaining the higher ground, for at once Anstis tensed like a bowstring.

'That is foolish speculation, Belstrang,' he said quickly. 'I urged you to withdraw, but you wouldn't listen. Such bullheadedness has put you in danger before, as I recall – but this time you overreach yourself. If I chose, I could-'

'You won't choose,' I broke in. 'I believe you were a party to Jessop's terrible scheme, though I've yet to find out why. A handsome payment, perhaps, from those disaffected Papists who still cling to hopes of regicide? Men like your own master, Sir Thomas Lake, who professes loyalty but attends masses in secret-'

'Stop your whoreson mouth!'

The words came like a whip-crack, cutting me short. His face flushed, Anstis strode round from behind his table, so that instinctively I was on my guard. But there was no assault: instead he hurried to close the door, then turned and stood with his back to it, staring angrily at me.

'Can you truly be such a fool, as to be unaware of the risks you run?' He demanded.'If you know whom I serve, then you must know I could have you snatched like a fly. And you can forget the legal fripperies, for there would be no trial: just a swift death, away from prying eyes. Do you follow?'

'I do,' I replied, steadying myself with an effort. 'And if I was uncertain before, I believe now that it was you who guided a deluded, angry youth in his purpose: paid him and encouraged him – and then when it all went awry, tried to cover your tracks. You sent men to Jane Rudlin's house to seize Jessop, but they were too late. Following which...' another thought struck me, making me catch my breath. 'Was it you who tried to have him poisoned in Bridewell – another failure, when someone else stole his food? Then, perhaps there was no need for a further attempt, since he'd lost his wits. He's set to die in Bedlam, which suits you perfectly: just another madman, whom no-one will mourn. Save that I've already told his family where he is, and asked leave to have him put in my charge – and his keeper knows it. Does that throw the matter into a different light?'

'God's heart…' Anstis sighed, shaking his head. 'I hoped it wouldn't come to this pass, Belstrang, but now you've tied my hands.'

He gave me a bleak look, of the kind I have seen often at the Assizes when a judge pronounces sentence. 'Why couldn't you have stayed in the country?' he muttered. 'Do you not see where you've put me?'

'Perhaps I should have told you sooner,' I lied, 'that I've engaged a servant, who's ready to ride up to Royston if I don't emerge within the hour. Your master's hunting with the King, is he not? I can imagine what will happen when my man delivers the letter I've prepared, for His Majesty's private perusal.'

But at that, some of Anstis's confidence returned. 'It's unwise to bluff, when you face a seasoned gamester,' he said. 'Few are reckless enough to do that with me.'

'Though you lost in the Low Countries, did you not?' I went on. 'Driven to desperate straits, I heard.' And when he stiffened again: 'I speak of your time as an intelligencer against Papists. Which puzzles me: for what possible reason could a man of your rank and religion have, for encouraging a Papist in his hare-brained attempt on the King's life? Unless the rewards were so great, that…'

I stopped abruptly; Anstis darted aside, and only then did I notice his sword in its scabbard, leaning against the wall. There was a shriek of steel, and the rapier was in his hand, levelled at my chest. In alarm, I placed my own hand on my sword-hilt… whereupon a laugh came up from somewhere, and burst from my mouth.

'What a rogue you are, after all,' I said, letting my hand fall. 'And since I'm no match for you, you have clear advantage. What will you do, run me through the heart, then call for men-at-arms? No doubt my own sword will be in my hand when they come, so you can claim self-defence. And given the lack of witnesses…'

I spread my hands - such defiance! In truth, I was torn: between the belief that Anstis would not dare to murder me in cold blood, and the possibility that he just might. For what seemed like an age we faced each other, until:

'There is, of course, another way,' he said.

With heart aflutter, I waited.

'You spoke of rewards,' he went on, with something of his old smoothness. 'Well, consider this: yours could be great – greater than you imagine. First, Sir Robert; then Baron Belstrang, with a seat in the Lords' Chamber. Later a viscountship perhaps, with a pension to match it.' He forced a thin smile. 'And properties too... there's one very near to yours, in Worcestershire: Sackersley, where your papist friend Jessop lives. The King has had his eye on it for Villiers, I hear. But on request, from the right quarters...' he lowered his sword until its tip touched the floor. 'Think on the choice I can offer, Belstrang; but think quickly, for I require a decision - now.'

I made no answer. My senses whirled - for despite all I knew of Anstis, I hadn't as yet thought him so base. This, I thought fleetingly, was one of the new breed of Whitehall schemers and sharpers George had ranted about: devoid of honour or scruples, and judging every man the same. To Anstis's mind, I could not fail to succumb.

'You're vermin,' I said at last. 'I'd rather cut my ears off than treat with you. Do what you will – the decision is yours, not mine.'

A look of surprise flitted across his features, to be replaced by one of grim resolution. Having pondered the matter since, I suppose I did not truly expect him to resort to the most desperate of measures, merely to silence a meddling old former justice like myself. But he was armed and vigorous, and driven close to desperation, while I was easy prey. I had just time to reflect on whether I had been too precipitate, when salvation appeared: the door opened abruptly, and Anstis's clerk looked in, wearing a concerned expression.

'Your pardon, sir...' he glanced from me to his master, who turned sharply, and back to me again. 'I heard... well, I was unsure what-'

'It's no matter – come in,' I said, letting out a breath. 'We were having a most interesting discourse, but I believe our business is done. Is that not so?'

The question was for Anstis, who was caught between anger and indecision; I had but a moment in which to take my leave, and I did not intend to waste it. I strode forward, forcing the clerk to step aside, then got myself out into the passage. Thereafter I lost no time in making for the door to New Palace Yard, cursing my decision to forgo Oldrigg's company. And in remarkably short order I was at the Stairs hailing a wherry.

Once on the water again, I had time to reflect that I had grown too old for that sort of confrontation; I could almost hear Childers chiding me for my rashness. Henceforth, I needed to think hard how to proceed, for there was no doubt that I had put myself in considerable danger. With this in mind I alighted at the Three Cranes in the Vintry and walked through the city by Royal Street, St Sythes Lane and Old Jewry, returning to Druett's house in the late afternoon. And here news awaited me: a letter from John Jessop, scrawled in haste and sent by courier to the Bel Savage, whence it had been brought by Oldrigg. As expected, it begged me to bring Thomas home, as speedily as I could.

And so, by the time Druett returned I was resolved: I would return to Bedlam the next morning, show the letter and demand Thomas's release. But when we sat together after supper, and I had related the day's events to him, my friend appeared subdued.

'I spoke to Jenner, the keeper of Bedlam,' he said. 'Not an easy man to find, nor was he inclined to aid me. In short, he refused utterly to reveal who pays for Thomas Jessop's board. He even claimed not to remember the youth, until I pressed him. If you wish for my opinion, the man's been told to keep his mouth closed - just as the fencing master was, and the drawer at the inn.' He gave a shake of his head. 'This is indeed a dark business. And from what you've told me today, I would counsel greater prudence.'

'Indeed?' I found myself frowning. 'Will you elaborate?'

'If I were a gamester, I'd put it in this fashion,' Druett said:

'Throw down your cards, and leave the table before you're ruined. This terrible anniversary plot you have uncovered – if it ever existed, of which I still have doubts – will bring you naught but trouble. For when all's said and done, no-one was harmed except the Jessop boy – and from what you've told me, his mind was afflicted before he even came to London. As for justice…' he sighed.

'Justice is a fugitive in these times, forever looking over its shoulder. Despite what I said to you last night, my advice is to throw off this burden, and return homeward.'

I stared at him, feeling as if a cold hand clutched my heart. *Have you too been warned?* I wanted to ask. *You, of all people?* At my expression, Druett frowned.

'Have I dismayed you?' he enquired.

'A little,' I replied after a moment. 'And as I said yesterday, I've no wish to draw you further into this business. I should find another place to lodge.'

His frown deepened. 'I've said there is no need. You're our honoured guest-'

'After I've got Jessop freed tomorrow,' I broke in, 'I'll need to house him somewhere while I make preparations to set forth to Worcestershire. I would not impose this on you and Frances… he might well be a trial to you both.'

Druett said nothing. And thinking upon my own words, I saw now that I had indeed assumed a difficult task in taking Thomas into my charge. Moreover, I was beholden to Druett for the money he had loaned me, and the debt he had discharged; was I judging him too harshly, I wondered?

'You must not think me ungrateful,' I went on. 'Without your aid, I could be dying of fever in the Compter. But it's best I act alone… I've stirred an anthill, and have no means of knowing who will be bitten.'

'Good Christ… is this you who speaks?'

He was regarding me, not with his advocate's face, but a look of disappointment. 'Do you think I mean to betray you?' And when I failed to answer: 'I spoke as a counsellor, not as a friend – will you doubt me so easily?'

'Then, speak as a friend,' I said tiredly. 'For I'm sorely in need of such.'

'As a friend who knows you, I say this,' came the sharp reply. 'Act according to your nature – as Justice Belstrang would. Free your poor Bedlam friend by all means, and get him to a place of safety. Then, and only then, should you decide: either to take him home, and leave the anthill, as you describe it – or to make another pass at your quarry, and obtain proof of who it was set the boy on such a terrible course. With proof, you can go to men who will listen – and no matter what station the plotters hold, there might be a chance of redress, however slim.' He paused, and drew breath. 'I know it's easy to say so in the privacy of my home, when it's you who bear the risk. But you're no stranger to that, are you?'

'And justice?' I asked, after a moment. 'This fugitive you spoke of, who fears its own shadow?'

'That was the lawyer speaking,' came the reply. 'But as your friend, I could argue that you're not alone in wanting evil-doers to pay for their crimes.' He raised his cup, and held it to his lips. 'To fugitives everywhere.'

To which I could only breathe my relief and join in the toast… whereupon another notion struck me, in the matter of Thomas's release. *A place of safety*, Druett had said – and at once, I knew where I should go.

THIRTEEN

The following morning I rode Leucippus out of the city by Moorgate, then took him by way of the Barbican and West Smithfield to Holborn, entering Shoe Lane from the north. Outside the Biershaws' house I dismounted, looking about for a boy to hold my horse. While I waited, I readied myself for my task, which was to persuade Henry Biershaw and his wife to lodge Thomas Jessop while I pursued my business.

I knew of no-one better suited to the task, though I was in no doubt about the magnitude of what I intended to ask. I would pay them of course, and offer what inducements I could, yet I knew I was counting on the innate good nature of a devout family; a Papist family. Once again, given my dealings with Jane Rudlin, and my employment of Oldrigg, I seemed to be involving myself with those of a religion I had hitherto despised; then, at risk of repeating myself, it was my Year of Astonishment. I was musing on this when a tug on my sleeve startled me.

''That's a fine horse, master... shall I mind him for you, while you go and seek the Gormand?'

I looked down at a boy, rough-haired and rough-clad, eying me expectantly.

'You shall,' I said. 'And there's a penny for you when I return. Though how do you know I'm seeking the Gormand?'

'That's what folk come for here for,' came the reply. 'To find Colley. Best keep hold of your hat, lest he eats it.'

With a dry look, I placed Leucippus's reins in his hand and knocked on the door. It was opened by Catherine Biershaw, who was taken aback.

'I hadn't thought to see you again, sir,' she began. 'And Henry's at his work...' whereupon my expression stayed her. 'Yet, you may speak with him if you wish.'

Leaving my horse and his holder, I followed her inside and along the passage to a door at the rear of the house. When she opened it, I was surprised: first by the strong light which came through tall windows, and then by the heat; the latter, I soon discerned, came from a small kiln by the wall. My next sensation was one of a mix of smells: linseed oil, gum Arabic, and others I failed to identify. I paused at the entrance, while Biershaw himself rose from a work-bench under the window, blinking at sight of me. Without further word his wife left us, and now I saw the gargantuan Colley by a small corner-shelf, concentrating fiercely upon cleaning something with a cloth. When I stepped forward he too looked up, then broke into a wide smile.

'Captain... you came again.' He dropped his cloth and came forward with his huge hand outstretched; in the other hand was a paintbrush. I returned his greeting, even as Biershaw came to his side.

'Go back to your work,' he said. 'While I speak with the gentleman.'

And when Colley obeyed, albeit with his smile fading, the glass-painter eyed me uneasily. 'I don't know what cause you have to come here again, sir,' he murmured. 'I thought our business was done.'

'It was,' I said. 'And I'm beholden for the aid you gave me. What I ask of you now is of a different nature, concerning our friend Philip.'

I had lowered my voice to an undertone to avoid Colley overhearing, but fortunately he appeared engrossed in his task. So without holding back, I spoke quickly to his father. I told him that the young man he knew as Philip Mayne was in Bedlam, wasting away and likely to die; that he was in torment, and was being cruelly treated; that his father had begged me to take him from there and bring him home to his family; and lastly that Philip had been led astray and used by unscrupulous men for their own purposes, leaving him broken. Having told all that I could, I stopped while my testimony sank home – but Biershaw's answer dismayed me.

He crossed himself, turning aside as he did so. Then he faced me and said: 'If it's God's will that he die there, so be it.'

'You misunderstand me,' I said. 'He was wrongly confined in Bridewell, where he fell into despair. Now he's held in Bedlam without good reason – he has harmed no-one. He needs to be back with the family who will cherish him, so that he may in time recover his wits.'

'The sin of despair brings its own reward,' Biershaw replied, refusing to meet my eye. 'It is not for you or I to question God's purpose, sir… and I do not understand why you bring this matter to me.'

'I came because you were a friend of his, and because I thought you might help him,' I replied, with some impatience. 'I mean to get Philip away from that place. I thought to ask you to lodge him for a night or two, while I make arrangements-'

'I cannot,' Biershaw broke in sharply. 'I have work to do – the first I've had in months. And we are busy with care of Colley…' He stopped himself, too late: Colley had ceased his brush-cleaning and was looking at us with interest.

'You are the only man of whom I can ask this, Master Biershaw,' I persisted. 'Philip has lived under your roof - he knows and trusts you. I would pay you for lodging him, for no longer than it takes me to finish my business. As a Christian man, will you not think on it?'

He made no reply to that; but if he was torn, there was no change in his demeanour. Glancing about the room, I saw a sheet of glass propped on the work-bench, and a partly-done painting upon it: an armorial crest of some kind, finely executed. The bench was untidy with tools, with pieces of glass and pots of colour. I was on the point of restating my case, when Colley spoke up.

'My father lets the sunlight, which is the light of God, into men's houses and so into their hearts,' he said.

'He does,' I agreed, my eyes on Biershaw. 'A worthy trade – and a gift.'

'See now, I have given you my answer, sir,' the glass-painter said. 'If it's God's will that the one you speak of stays where he is, I will not gainsay it.'

I sighed, my patience disappearing. 'I cannot think God such a varlet that he would let that young man perish in the madhouse,' I answered. 'More likely, I suspect He would help those who wish to help others…'

I stopped as Biershaw drew back. 'I'll not hear such talk in my house,' he said – then he stiffened: his son was moving his great frame towards us.

'Philip's my friend,' he announced. 'Will he come again?'

'I cannot say, Colley,' I replied.

'We would talk of angels,' he went on. 'The angels of the seven days...'

'That's enough,' Biershaw broke in. 'Have you done the brushes? I'll need them soon.'

Colley's face fell, and for a moment I feared a repeat of the behaviour I had witnessed on my first visit there: his distress, and his bizarre habit of eating anything that came to hand. Instead he backed away, his eyes still upon me.

'I know that I ask a great deal,' I said to Biershaw. 'But I ask it for Philip, not for myself. He will die alone – to be buried without your sacred rites,' I added, as the thought sprang to mind. 'If it's within your power, would you not wish to remedy that?'

He was silent, his face grim on a sudden - and in truth I felt shamed by the way I had pressed him. Glancing at Colley I saw he was ill-at-ease, sensing discord. With a heavy heart, I thought it best to abandon my efforts and go elsewhere; the notion of returning to Jane Rudlin even occurred. I was about to leave, when the glass-painter gave a sigh, and spoke up.

'You say you ask me as a Christian man, sir,' he said, blinking at me in that way he had. 'Do you regard yourself as such?'

'Does it matter?' I asked him.

'To me it does.'

'Well then, I was born a Protestant,' I answered. 'But in truth, I'm no longer a man of deep faith. Too much reading, perhaps - and too much observance of the fickleness of those who profess piety. Then, are you yourself not obliged to attend a church every week, and take part in a liturgy that means nothing to you, merely because you are forced by law?'

'I speak not of that,' Biershaw replied, with a shake of his head. 'I want to understand why you are intent on helping one of our religion. Do you see yourself as the Samaritan – or have you some other cause?'

I hesitated; both father and son were watching me. 'I have no cause other than to see justice carried,' I said finally.

'That smacks of atheism,' Biershaw said, his face clouding.

'I would not say so,' I answered. 'Rather, I incline towards the thinking of the ancients – of a man called Pyrrho of Elis. His followers were called *skeptics* – it means those who look about them without passion, who observe and consider.'

There was silence then, as he did some considering of his own. Then he sighed, and said: 'I don't have your learning, sir. Yet I can see that even you might be a part of God's plan in this matter. If Philip is in such grave danger, as you say - and I do not disbelieve you – then our maker may have laid this duty upon me too, to see him taken back to his father's house.'

I said nothing, though my hopes lifted.

'Yet in one regard you are mistook,' Biershaw resumed: 'this is not a place of safety. Our neighbours are good people for the most part, but there are others who eye our every move, and would not scruple to inform on us for reward, however paltry. Some are mere children, egged on by their fathers. You understand me?'

'I do,' I answered, my thoughts going to the boy who was minding Leucippus. 'Yet it is no crime to succour a fellow man in need of shelter. Philip will remain under my protection, and I will answer any charges.'

After a moment the man nodded, upon which I offered him my heartfelt thanks. Whereupon Colley, who had been still throughout our discourse, took a step forward again. 'Will you bring Philip here, Captain?' he asked, a smile forming.

'If he will come,' I told him. To Biershaw I said: 'I mean to go there at once, and bring him back on my horse. Will you speak to your wife, or shall I explain the matter to her?'

'I'll do what's needed,' Biershaw said. 'You should go now, sir, and do the part you seem to cherish: that of rescuer.'

I gave a nod, ready to take my leave, but instead I paused. I looked into the face of a good and kindly man, and shamed myself for the deception I still practised. I was done with dissembling, of the kind I had used with Anstis.

'There is something more I should tell you,' I said. 'Our

friend's true name is not Philip Mayne; he used that for secrecy's sake, and so as not to endanger others. In time, if he chooses to speak, he may tell you himself. It's my hope that he will.'

And I left him then, in the workshop that let the sunlight in.

Now a haste was upon me, for it was a week since I had seen Thomas. When I paid my horse-holder I barely looked at him, but took the reins and climbed into the saddle. Biershaw's words rang in my head: could even this seemingly carefree child be an informant? As I turned the horse, I saw his eyes fixed curiously upon me, and was reminded at once of my own present danger: if I were watched since my encounter with Antis the day before – which seemed likely - was a return to Bedlam a risk both for myself, and for Thomas? I resolved at once to engage Oldrigg to help me see the boy safely delivered. Beyond that, I had only a vague notion of what I would do. As for my talk with Druett and its implications... I forced the thought aside, and urged Leucippus to a trot, up to Holborn Bridge and back through West Smithfield.

Oldrigg was phlegmatic about my mission; to him it was just another foray, and he the hired protector. While I rode, he walked beside me through Moorfields, wet and marshy from the rains, until we emerged via Petty France into Bishopsgate Street and so arrived at the doors of Bedlam. I dismounted, and he stood by Leucippus while I called for the porter. But when at last one appeared it was not Scantbury but another man, of a quite different stamp: tall and spindle-thin, with lank hair about his ears. At his belt was an oak billet, which looked somewhat too well-used for my liking. When I asked for Scantbury, the man shook his head.

'He's busy, sir. Will you state your business?'

He glanced at Oldrigg, who was watching him stonily. Striving not to appear in too much haste, I took Jessop's letter from my pocket and handed it to the man, whereupon the first difficulty presented itself; he was unable to read.

'I never took to schooling,' he said, handing it back. 'What does it say?'

I told him briefly, embroidering my account with mention of a visit to Thomas Jenner, which had in truth been Druett's and not mine; already I was dissembling again. But even as I laid out my case, the man lifted his hand in refusal.

'It's not my place to release an inmate,' he said. 'I fear your journey is wasted.'

Impatiently I held the letter up before his face. 'It's signed by his father, a landowner from my county named John Jessop-'

I caught my breath, too late; and here was the second difficulty.

'Who?' The porter demanded. 'I thought you came for Philip Mayne.'

'I do,' I said, cursing my carelessness. 'It's another name he uses…'

'Does he?' The man regarded me suspiciously. 'It's the first time I've heard it.'

'Yet it's no matter,' I said, pummelling my mind for effective argument. 'I'm a former justice and a lawyer, who will answer for his actions before any court in London. I have leave to take that young man away from here, before he starves himself to death - it's but an act of charity, to restore him to his family. So - will you bring him to me, or must I summon a sergeant-at-mace to assist me?' And thinking fast, I added: 'I might even serve a warrant on you, for resisting an order.'

At that the man blanched. He had not the wit or stolidity of Scantbury; nor, I recalled, had Scantbury found it necessary to carry a billet. Seeing a chink in the fellow's defences, I caught Oldrigg's eye. He understood at once, and stepped forward to stand an arm's length from the porter. And though the man was taller than Oldrigg by an inch, he was no more his match than I was, with my sixty-one years. He flinched, and his hand dropped to his belt.

'There are orders,' he said, 'which I can't gainsay… you've no cause to press me.'

'I haven't even begun to press you,' I said in an innocent tone. 'And what's your name, pray?'

'It's… that's of no import,' the other said, wiping a hand across his mouth. 'You did ask for Scantbury… perhaps it's best

I go and find him.'

'Perhaps it is,' I said, whereupon he turned speedily towards the doors. As he went, however, he spoke over his shoulder.

'Only, he'll tell you the same,' he said with a scowl. 'And you've no right, coming here making threats.'

He was gone, and Oldrigg and I stood without speaking while the Bishopsgate traffic passed us by. He, I saw, wore a look of disdain at the way the tall man had taken fright so readily; clearly, he had no time for the turnkeys of Bedlam. And when the figure of Scantbury emerged some minutes later he frowned, at which I gave him a quick shake of my head.

'You wish to speak with me, sir,' Scantbury said, stopping a short distance away. 'Did you want to see your friend again?'

'A deal more than that,' I replied. 'Do you recall my promise, when we last met?'

Once again I told my business, and again I showed Jessop's letter, contriving to conceal the signature. But to my annoyance, Scatbury refused even to look at it.

'It's of no use, sir,' he said, in his phlegmatic voice. 'We've had orders since you came here, that Philip is not to be freed. Hence I won't aid you.'

'Orders from whom?' I demanded.

'I cannot say, sir,' he answered with a shrug. 'But it's not uncommon. The boy's a danger to others.'

'That's untrue, and you know it,' I snapped. 'Even if it were, there's a man here who's equal to the task of handling Philip. I have lodgings arranged, as well as leave from his father to place the boy in my care. Since he is not yet of age…'

'The age is of no consequence,' Scantbury interrupted. 'He's a madman, who must be confined.' He stood his ground, hands at his sides. 'Your pardon, but I cannot aid you,' he said again. Then he put his fingers to his mouth, and gave a loud whistle. At once the doors of the hospital opened, and the beanpole of a porter re-emerged, billet in hand. Nervously he approached, to stand by Scantbury.

For a while we looked at each other, until Oldrigg decided he had had enough. He started forward, whereupon I was obliged to grasp his arm.

'There will be no affray,' I said, as the other men responded: Scantbury reached for his poniard, while his companion raised his billet. Lifting a hand, I bade them desist. Finally, when Oldrigg was still, I eyed Scantbury.

'Will you at least let me talk to Philip?' I asked. 'I mean as before, alone in the churchyard. You may keep a watch, if you will.'

'Why of course, sir,' came the reply, and with it an expression that I read clearly enough: once again money must change hands. 'If you'd care to go to the same place, I will meet you there.'

He looked pointedly at his companion, who with some relief went inside. As soon as he was gone Scantbury turned expectantly, while I opened my purse. But when I proffered three pennies, he shook his head.

'Four pence is the charge, sir, nothing less.'

With a frown I paid, and it was done; Oldrigg stayed with Leucippus while I passed through the wicket-gate once more, down the mudded lane to Bedlam churchyard. This time the place was not deserted, a labourer being at work in the far corner, digging a grave. Uneasily I made my way to the rotting bench near the hospital wall and waited until the door opened as before, and Scantbury appeared leading his charge by the arm. But at sight of Thomas, I gave a start: he was stumbling weakly, and on his cheek below the left eye was a large, yellowing bruise.

'What's this?' I demanded of the porter. 'Has he been beaten?'

'It's naught, sir,' was the calm reply. 'A tussle with another distracted fellow...' he looked at Thomas, whose eyes were on the ground. 'Is that not so, Philip?'

There was no answer of course; and with a heavy heart I steeled myself for another wasted visit. Scantbury told Thomas to sit, then walked off to the corner of the churchyard where he began a leisurely conversation with the grave-digger; it was clear that, this time, he would remain there for the duration. Whereupon I sat down beside the youth I had promised to have released, searching for words that might have some effect –

until I was confounded.

'I know why you've come, Master Belstrang,' Thomas Jessop said softly.

I caught my breath and looked sharply at him. The face was as I remembered from our last meeting: drawn and pale, with the added blemish of the ugly bruise. But the eyes met mine, with as bleak a look as I have ever seen.

'Heaven be praised...' unthinkingly I put out a hand to grasp his, but he did not respond. 'You cannot know what it means to hear you speak,' I added.

He regarded me, then spoke hoarsely, as in a voice that had long been in disuse. 'You're a good man... my father thought so, even when you once levelled a fine upon him. But you should go now, for I'll not leave this place.'

'And yet, it's for your father's sake that I'm here,' I said - 'his and your mother's.' I pulled the letter from my sleeve, but Thomas was shaking his head.

'I will never see them again,' he said. 'I must pay for my sins, and let my maker's will be done.'

'Listen to me,' I said urgently. 'I have spoken to people you know – Jane Rudlin, Henry Biershaw and others. I believe-'

'I know,' he broke in, cutting me short. 'I heard all that you said, the last time.'

'You heard me?' I echoed, striving to understand. 'Then why did you not speak, when we were alone? I came to help you...'

'You did,' came the reply. 'And I've prayed for a blessing upon you. It was a kindly act...' He trailed off, and his gaze shifted to the other side of the churchyard where Scantbury stood. 'Likely that one is for me,' he murmured.

He meant the grave. Fumbling for words of remonstrance, I opened his father's letter and held it up, but he merely looked away.

'I fear I am beyond mercy in this life,' he said. 'For in my foolishness I did the bidding not of the heavenly father, but of the Evil One. I should have seen his servant for what he was, but I was blind.'

'His servant?' I frowned at him. 'Who was that?'

'His name is Anstis,' came the reply. Then, with a sigh:

'And he had marked me out for his instrument, before I even left Sackersley.'

FOURTEEN

That night after supper Druett and I had another discourse, with a deal of sober reflection on both our parts. Thomas Jessop's testimony had shaken the two of us – but Druett's news shook me to the bone.

Edmund Anstis was dead.

'He was found this morning in the river, close to the Parliament Stairs,' Druett said. 'Drowned, they say - but I don't believe it. Nor will you, I expect.'

I was confounded, my harsh encounter with the man still fresh in my mind; and yet I was even more dismayed by what had happened since. For, with a heavy heart, I had been obliged to leave Thomas at Bedlam once again, which made my ride back a grim and solitary one. I had sent Oldrigg to the Biershaws to tell them their guest would not come after all, while I had time to think on his tale; I might call it his confession, of his temptation into evil-doing. Hours later, having recounted it to Druett, I still viewed it with mingled anger and disbelief.

It had begun last summer, Thomas told me, in a voice filled with shame. The man he later knew as Anstis had, it seemed, heard of Thomas and deemed him most suited for a device he and others had in mind. Contriving to get Thomas alone, far away from eavesdroppers, he amazed the boy with a vision of what could be done – and of an England that might come to be. He told him that there were many who thought privately as he did, who hated the heretic King James and wished to see him gone. Only then could the process begin: to restore the true and proper religion, as the martyrs of 1605 had tried and failed to do. The tenth anniversary of their bold attempt was approaching; what better time to carry out the just and rightful removal of the tyrant? And he, Thomas Jessop, could be the one to carry it through!

Thomas was both amazed and terrified, he admitted, but Anstis was a most persuasive man, who had prepared his case skilfully. Thomas would not only be a hero, doing God's work in this way: he would be a saint. Catholics throughout England would honour him and revere his name, and that of the father and mother who bore him too. No longer would they suffer fines and cruel repression, but would be free to worship in the one true faith – to attend mass and go to confession as they wished, without fear of reprisal. The king's son and heir would convert to Catholicism - and when the Prince married the Spanish Infanta, the great Roman world of mystery and miracle, that had been under the Protestant yoke for so long, would by the grace of God be rebuilt, and all would rejoice!

'I was mortally afraid,' Thomas told me hoarsely, with one eye on his keeper. 'I struggled to believe that I could be the means of bringing about such momentous change. But he worked upon me, did Anstis, until I could find no words to gainsay him. I had been observed and noted, he told me; I was steadfast and noble, fit for greater things than to languish unhappily in the shire of my birth. And I would have help, he said, from good and devout people. I could kill the King at Whitehall - as the serpent should perish in its own lair, where so much evil had been concocted. On the fifth of November, when the Powder Sermon was preached before the King by the anniversarist bishop, I would be in the palace disguised as a servant, in royal livery. Another man would contrive to bring me into the chapel, close enough to the royal seat – then, while the heads of the King and those about him were bowed in prayer, I would run at him with a poniard that had been hidden inside my clothing. I was to be shown how to stab the King in the neck, avoiding his collar and his padded doublet – it would be swift, and death would soon follow. Thereafter, in the uproar and confusion, I would be seized and spirited away by accomplices, got outside to the river stairs where a boat would be waiting. I would be taken to safety, there to gather with others of the faith, and a priest would hear my confession and offer succour. By then, of course, the King's Council would have been spurred to action – but the setters-on had planned carefully, to the effect that there would be no hue and cry for me.'

Here Thomas had paused in his testimony, and with a great

sigh added that this was the part he had struggled with most, that had caused him days and nights of torment. 'A dupe,' he said, his eyes on the ground. 'A slow-witted fellow who bore a passing resemblance to me, would be dressed identically to me and introduced within the palace walls. My accomplices – whom I did not know, it being safer that way – would claim to have seized the fanatic in his attempt to escape, and would hand him over to men-at-arms: another Ravaillac, bound for a terrible death. But when I balked at that - that another should pay so heavily for my sin - Anstis had his argument ready: a priest would give the man absolution, he said, for his part in the removal of the tyrant. The substitute assassin would die a martyr. And I -' this with a most woeful look – 'like the fool I was, I believed him. I believed him all through those months, when I came to London and was tutored for my role – with a new name, chosen by Anstis. It was fitting, he said, that I should take the surname of Cuthbert Mayne, one of the bravest of our martyrs. And so, I complied - until the very day arrived, and I learned the truth.'

And when I asked him how he had learned it, he had begun to weep.

'They were preparing me, on that morning of the fifth, in a private house,' he said miserably. 'Two people I did not know: a man who served Anstis and who supplied me with the poniard, and a woman who was to dress my hair and fit me out in the King's livery; I had already been instructed how to carry myself. Even then I did not suspect that deception was being done – until I asked after the dupe who was to be clothed like me, and saw the look on the woman's face. This one mistake - this tiny slip - was what saved the King's life, and allowed me to see in that moment that it was all a wicked device. There was no other livery, the woman said, and who was this dupe? Then I saw the way the man looked angrily at her, and I knew: I was the dupe! The instrument... and the biggest fool in all England. I was the one who must kill the king and be arrested for it - perhaps killed then and there, so I could not testify against others. The movers would escape, and I would have served their purpose. And if Anstis had lied to me about that...'

In despair, he put his head in his hands. 'I demanded to see him, and was told I could not. And I saw something else, then: that these people were not of my faith as they pretended. And if they were not, then neither was Anstis, though he had claimed otherwise. He had used me from the beginning, though to this day I do not understand why. I have prayed and racked myself since, day and night, but God has not seen fit to give me an answer.'

He had looked up, with a face of anguish. 'The blindfold was torn from my eyes,' he told me. 'I saw then that I had not served God or Christ, or the Holy Father in Rome, or my faith, but Satan - at which I fled in torment from the house where we were. I ran by myriad ways until I fetched up at Mistress Jane's, by which time…'

He sagged, a broken reed. 'What followed, Master Belstrang, I think you know.'

He was done, and I had no words of comfort, nor even of censure. Soon after that I had left him slumped on the bench and got myself back to Bishopsgate Street where, seeing my expression, Oldrigg eyed me curiously. I was as one bereft; I felt as if my mission to see Thomas freed and returned to his family was not only stalled, but without reason or hope. Perhaps Jane Rudlin was right, I thought: that it was best he died in Bedlam after all, a distracted youth who had intended to commit a heinous crime but failed to carry it out, simply because a careless tiring-woman had made a slip of the tongue.

And when I had relayed the whole sorry tale to Druett, he could only agree. Now, with the news of Anstis's death coming hard upon it, we were at a loss.

'All of Whitehall knows of it,' my friend said, after we had sat in silence for a while. 'Soon the King will return from Royston for the Easter festival, and the rest of his Council will hear, Sir Thomas Lake among them... I wonder what that sly weasel will make of his minion's sudden demise.'

'You're still certain Lake couldn't have had any role in this wicked scheme?' I asked, to which Druett shook his head.

'It's impossible. I've told you, the man would have no part in any plot against the King. He has succeeded in rising to the highest office alongside Winwood, hence he hasn't the need – or the nerve - for such skulduggery. Moreover, he would know his name would be tarnished whether he knew of it or not, because of his faith. He'd be thrown in the Tower, along with Northumberland and the rest.'

'Then in God's name, why would Anstis undertake such a bold stratagem?'

'Money?' Druett suggested. 'He's a gambler... likely he had debts.'

'But the risk,' I muttered, to which my friend merely sighed.

'Perhaps someone had intelligence enough to threaten him. He's been reckless in the past...' He broke off. 'But I speculate, and these are straws in the wind.'

We fell silent again. It was late, Frances was already abed, and from the street outside the watchman's cry could be heard. I was as low in spirits as I had been from the start of this affair, seeing no way open to me - except to throw the whole business over and go back home. I might even have done so, had John Jessop's face not stuck in my mind, that cold afternoon at Thirldon when he pleaded for my help. It was a mere two weeks back, though it seemed like months.

'What will you do now?' Druett asked, breaking my reverie.

'In truth, I do not know,' I told him.

'Then my only advice is to sleep on it, if you can.'

I did sleep a little that night, being mighty tired by events. Towards dawn I awoke with a start, the picture of a forlorn Thomas Jessop etched hard in my mind. Vague thoughts sprang up: of contriving to bribe the Keeper of Bedlam to release him, even against his will, and have Oldrigg help me bring him away; of seeking a private audience with someone in authority – a member of the Privy Council, say – and telling all; or once again, of leaving the whole fearful business behind, which meant abandoning Thomas to a lonely and wretched death... until, finally, came the only notion that appealed just then. I would ride out to Highgate once more, as I had promised, and spend a little time with my daughter and grand-daughter. It seemed the only thing worth rising from my bed for.

Having taken breakfast, and seen Druett leave for Westminster in a somewhat grim humour, I saddled Leucippus myself and rode out by Cripplegate, then through Islington to Highgate on the hill, to George Bull's house. But from the moment I was greeted by Anne and brought inside, I sensed that all was not well. Kate was with her nurse, she said, and I would see her presently, but just now she wished to talk... or rather George did. And when I showed my surprise, her husband himself appeared from his private room and, after a perfunctory greeting, invited me to sit. To my further surprise, Anne left us.

'What in heaven's name is amiss?' I asked as soon as we were alone, for my son-in-law wore a forbidding look. 'And how did you know I was coming here?'

'I had hopes you might tell me what's amiss, Master Justice,' George said, in a manner cool and distant. 'And I had no inkling that you were intending to visit today - but it's apt, for I would have sought you out.' He paused, then: 'I've heard troubling news at Westminster. In particular, I learn that two days ago you attacked one of the Council's secretaries in his chamber, and had to be removed from the Palace.'

'Do you, now?' I said, after a moment. 'And you believe that?'

'I've tried my best not to,' was his reply. 'I was hoping you would enlighten me further.' He hesitated, then: 'It's become a matter of importance, given that the same man was found dead in the Thames yesterday morning.'

'By God...' I stared at him. 'What, do you think I killed him?'

'Of course not,' George said, with some impatience. 'Yet I'm eager to know what your relations were with him.'

'Yes... I can see why,' I said, somewhat heavily. I had been so bound up in my affairs of late, only then did it occur to me that someone like George could have heard rumours. 'And you fear those relations could throw suspicion on-'

'On us all,' George broke in. 'I think you know what I speak of: Edmund Anstis was not a man of good reputation – I would even say he was a man without honour, despite having risen to a position of trust.'

'As secretary to Sir Thomas Lake...'

'Under-secretary,' George corrected. 'Though his loyalties have at times been questioned – but we digress.' He drew a breath, then: 'Will you not tell me, your son by marriage, what lies behind this business? For if rumours are allowed to flourish unchecked, you may find yourself facing questions – even arrest. Surely you can see how it appears?

'Perhaps so,' I said, coming to the view that George at least deserved an explanation. How and where to begin, however, was a most taxing thought.

'Then speak, sir, I pray you,' he said, allowing his precisian manner to surface. 'For as matters stand, it appears to me you've acted in a most careless and unseemly way for a man of your station.'

I confess my hackles were rising now, to the point where I might have acted more precipitately than I should. George the prosecutor was not a man I wanted to face – nor, I felt, should I be shamed by one such as he.

'Let me reassure you on one count, at the least,' I said. 'It was not I who attacked Edmund Anstis, but he who drew his sword against me. His clerk, whose interruption was, to use your word, fortuitous, would stand witness to that...' I paused. 'Or, perhaps he wouldn't.'

'But why did Anstis do so?' George enquired. 'What was the cause?'

I gave a sigh; I have said before that I was tired of dissembling. Recalling my last visit here, when Anne dissuaded me from speaking of my involvement with the Jessop family, I was torn between more evasion and telling the truth. Surely even George, I thought, would see the injustice of it, and the way Anstis had worked to thwart me, almost from the moment of my arrival in London? But to my further displeasure, he took my silence for some kind of guilt.

'Why won't you speak?' he demanded. 'What am I to think of this cloudy business? Have you forgotten the oaths you took, and your time on the Justice's bench? Anne is distressed by the news, though I've been at pains to assure her of your-'

'My what?' I said, cutting him short. 'My good name? I need no lessons in propriety from you, Master Bull.'

'Indeed?' On a sudden George was on his feet, and at his most officious. 'Then if not me, sir, it would appear that you need lessons from someone.'

'By heaven...' Scarcely aware of it, I too rose to my feet. 'You've not the least notion what I do,' I said, with heat. 'I've not sought to do mischief to anyone – quite the contrary. I came from home to see my daughter and my grandchild and mend the bonds between us, and to make some enquiries on a neighbour's behalf. Though I wish to God I'd never listened to the man when I did, let alone acted so impulsively, given the trials I have been put to...'

I stopped as the door opened. There was Anne, wearing a most anxious expression, drawn by our raised voices. Seeing both George and I standing, seemingly railing at one another, she blanched; and when George turned about, I assumed to tell her to leave us, I lost my control.

'See now, I'm truly sick with all of this,' I exclaimed. 'I'm weary of treading on hot coals, as I am with being threatened, with being given the lie, with racking myself for actions done and not done – and with being judged!'

They were silent, gazing at me: Anne in dismay, George puzzled and angry. Then, through the open doorway, came a sound that sent my heart tumbling: Kate began to cry, doubtless frightened by my shouting.

I sat down again, my head bowed in shame. And only when the crying ceased, from the sound of it by means of the nurse's ministrations, did I look up.

'I will tell you everything,' I said, my eyes on George. 'And when I'm finished, you may decide whether you wish me to remain in your house or not. So, are you ready to listen?'

It took less time than I feared, and when I ended my testimony both George and Anne were seated, struck dumb by the tale. I believe I understood then the appeal of Confession: now that all was in the open I felt relieved and unburdened, if unsure how they would respond. Anne, true to her nature, was concerned for me, and distressed to learn of my imprisonment in the Compter. George, for different reasons, was appalled.

'Why did you not get word to me?' He asked. 'Did you think I would leave you there to take infection, or worse? Do you think so badly of me as that?'

'I do not, and did not,' I told him. 'I feared to bring disgrace upon you… though in truth, you appear to think I have done so anyway.'

He stood up then, not angrily, but needing to move about as he considered the matter. Once he stopped as if to speak, then thought better of it. Anne, sitting close to me, put her hand on my arm.

'You should not have taken on the Jessops' burden,' she said. 'It has brought you nothing but trouble and humiliation – and danger too. And yet…' she sighed, and almost smiled. 'It's a comfort to see you haven't lost your instinct for justice.'

'Justice?' At that, George turned to face us. 'He has become embroiled with Papists, to the extent of flouting the law.'

'Well, I suppose I have,' I answered, having no stomach for further raillery. 'And I'll allow that my desire to know what put Thomas Jessop in such a plight has led me to rashness. But I've learned that the youth was beguiled, duped into taking part in an action that even he never contemplated, until Anstis ensnared him…'

'Yes, you have told us.' George interrupted. Whereupon, seemingly having arrived at a decision, he sat down facing me. 'And now you must tell others.'

For a moment I was unsure of his meaning, until it dawned upon both Anne and me at the same time. 'Now who is acting rashly?' she said at once. 'This matter needs weighing carefully, before anyone hurries to a decision.'

'I have weighed it already,' George answered. 'Surely you see the gravity of it? Your father has just told of an attempted regicide – another Papist plot. The fact that it did not take place is immaterial – the plotters must be found and brought to trial. They cannot be left at large, to regroup and devise some new stratagem.'

He was in full righteous humour, and I could not gainsay him.

Though he was no admirer of King James, the notion of another attempt on the monarch's life, with all the turmoil that could bring, both outraged and frightened him. The fact of Anstis's death added fuel to the flames; seemingly the man had been working in consort with others, for reasons yet to be discovered. As if to give voice to my thoughts, George spoke up again.

'Do you think that was why Anstis was killed?' he asked. 'For from what I hear, no-one thinks this a simple matter of drowning while drunk, as it was made to appear. Perhaps he was slain in order to silence him, if he was deemed to pose a risk to someone. Whatever the case, we must act swiftly before suspicion falls upon you, who quarrelled with him. The fact that you have been mingling with known Papists will count against you. Yet we must go together, and lay the whole sorry business forth, for good or ill.'

'You and I?' I shook my head. 'I've no desire to involve you further. Let me speak with John Druett again, and decide how best to proceed.'

'No, sir, that will not do.'

George was adamant, and seeing Anne about to speak, he silenced her with a glance. ''You have confided in me – and I believe all that you've said - but there must be no delay,' he went on. 'There is a man I trust completely, who will hear your testimony and who will know how to act: Sir Edward Coke, the Chief Justice.'

I frowned at that. Coke: the one who had tried the Powder Plotters a decade ago, and sentenced them to the harshest of deaths; in his sixties now, but still vigorous – and a man after George's heart. Only now, perhaps, did I see the matter as George viewed it: another terrible, if failed, attempt on the King's life, which could be talked of for years to come. Whereupon a new thought occurred – or rather, it leaped to my mind with such force, I could not help but voice it.

'This would be a good opportunity for you, would it not?' I said. 'To do your part in uncovering what may be known as the Anniversary Plot...' I glanced at Anne. 'You may even find yourself styled Lady Bull, wife to Sir George.'

'Father!' Anne was aghast. 'How can you think so? It's most cruel of you.'

I looked away, but having conceived the notion, I could not dismiss it. George, for his part, bristled like a cockerel, and to all appearances he and I were about to do battle again. Instead he reined himself in, breathing hard, then:

'Do you truly think that is my only motive, sir?'

'I can only hope that it isn't,' I replied.

'Well then, there's no more to be said,' was his response.' You may choose to come with me to the Chief Justice or not. But in either event, I will go this afternoon to Westminster and tell him all. So, will you take a drink before you leave, or will you stay to dinner, before we leave together?'

FIFTEEN

I did stay to eat a simple meal with George and Anne, but not for the reason they thought. I was heavy of heart, for I knew that if the whole matter were put before Sir Edward Coke, one of the Privy Councillors, that would be the end of Thomas Jessop. By his very act of contemplation, the boy had condemned himself as a regicide. It was George who quoted the words of the Chief Justice to me *verbatim*, from the man's own writings on treason, as if delivering a sermon:

'If diverse do conspire the death of the King, and the manner how, and provide weapons or the like for the execution of the conspiracy, this is a sufficient overt act to prove the compassing and imagination of the death of the King.'

He sat back from the table, as one who has made his case. And when I said nothing, he added: 'I cannot share in your pity for that wicked youth. The fact that he was prevented from action – no doubt by God's timely intervention – does not excuse him.'

'And nor, in your eyes, does insanity,' I said.

Instead of replying George was silent for a while. And when he spoke again, it was on a different matter.

'I was there at the trials, at the end of 1605, in Westminster Hall,' he said quietly. 'A novice lawyer from the Temple, agog at the gravity of it all. I saw Fawkes and the others, and marvelled at their base treachery. Along with my fellows I heard the evidence in horror, that such a treasonous plot could have been hatched – not by Spaniards or any agent of Rome, but by trueborn Englishmen like Catesby and Rookwood and the Wintours - even a knight like Digby. The consequences of that explosion, if it had come to pass, were beyond my imagination: The King and Queen dead, the bishops and Councillors - and to crown it all, there was no repentance from the plotters. They went to the gallows and the butcher's block, those serpents, in the same mind as when they placed the barrels of powder under the Lords' chamber and laid the fuse. And now?' He looked fiercely at me. 'You wish to let Jessop escape justice, by reason of feebleness of mind? To my thinking it was his own wickedness, when once he realised the import of what he was about to do, that put him in Bedlam.'

'Many would say such,' I allowed. 'But I've known him from childhood. He was restless and troubled, seeing how his mother and father suffered, seeking some purpose to his life as a Catholic beyond mere obedience to the King's laws, as the Archpriest urged - as the Pope himself urged. Such meekness is beyond some men. The worse crime, to my mind, was done by those like Anstis, who saw him for the malleable youth he was: as his father put it to me, one fit for impression. They trained him as an unruly colt, and brought him to the deed, so he would pay the price for it while they kept in the shadows. And hence…'

I stopped: I was resolved, I knew then, as I had been all along. Looking at Anne and George in turn, I laid out my position: I could not, and would not let Thomas die in the madhouse.

'Very well, sir,' George said, after a long moment. 'I will wait while you decide on your course of action, but only until tomorrow morning. If you are not here by ten of the clock, I'll go to Coke alone and tell him all that you have told me.'

Seeing that he too was resolved, I had little choice but to comply.

That afternoon, through showers of rain I rode to Westminster and spent time seeking out Druett, who had business with a wayward client: one of those dissolute rakes who are afraid to leave the sanctuary of Whitehall for fear of being arrested for debt. By the time he was free the day had worn on, and being weary, he was somewhat short with me. But he agreed to take a drink in the alehouse by King Street, which is frequented by Whitehall Palace servants and the like. There, over a mug of tepid spiced ale, I told him what had occurred.

'By all that's holy,' he breathed, after some reflection. 'Your predicament appears to worsen with each day that passes. How do you propose to manage this?'

'In truth, I scarcely know,' I said. 'But if there's one thing I wish to do before I confront the fearsome Coke – which I suppose I must - it's to get Thomas Jessop out of Bedlam. Otherwise he faces torture to reveal whatever he knows, followed by a terrible death. Despite what he's done, I do not believe he merits that.'

'Yet, even if it were possible to free him, you would put yourself in severe jeopardy by it,' Druett said with a frown. 'You would be abetting a confessed regicide.'

'The intended regicides were Anstis and those who set him on,' I countered. 'Thomas was but their instrument-'

'It's enough,' Druett interrupted. 'You know as well as I that Coke and the rest of the Council won't see it in that way – he's guilty before he's even brought to trial.' He sighed, then: 'My counsel is to give up this ambition and to go with Bull tomorrow. Give your account, and plead what circumstances you can. If the Chief Justice is feeling merciful, he may approve your actions in uncovering this Anniversary Plot, as you call it. If not, he'll have you arraigned for complicity or some such, and impose a heavy fine at the very least.'

I looked down at the table: old, scarred, and stained with years of use, somewhat like the Robert Belstrang who viewed it, I thought. Again, the weight of this unholy business sat heavily upon me. Druett's advice was sound: the truth was out now that I had told George, and matters would soon be taken from my hands. I drank my spiced ale, and faced the fact that Thomas would not be returning to his father's house in Worcestershire. Indeed, the whole notion looked as if it had been fanciful from the beginning.

'I ask your pardon once more, for drawing you into this mire,' I said.

'You should ask it of Frances,' Druett said. 'It's she who urged me along in this matter.' He paused, then: 'She adored you once, though you seemed not to notice.'

'You're mistaken,' I said, meeting his gaze. 'I chose not to notice. You were the man she needed, who would give her what I could not.'

'Well… and here we are, more than thirty years on.'

'Here we are.'

We sat and drained our mugs, but when the drawer came to ask if we wanted them refilled, Druett waved him away. 'I'm for home,' he said. 'Are you coming with me?'

For a while I did not reply; a notion had taken root, which on the face of it was foolhardy in the extreme. Without warning, Childers' gloomy countenance came to my mind, as if to warn me of my folly; I had not written to him or to Hester for what seemed a long time. But there, once again, was the careworn face of John Jessop... on a sudden, I banged my fist down on the table.

'That worm of a keeper, Jenner,' I said. 'If he hadn't made difficulties, the boy could have been freed from Bedlam yesterday.'

'Those associates of Anstis – the setters-on, if you will – must have pressed the man,' Druett said. 'Likely they got rid of Anstis too, because he was a danger to them... and they watch your movements still. Why would they not?' He frowned. 'I wonder if they'll let you get to Coke, to spill your tale - had you thought on that?'

'I confess I had not,' I said, as the notion struck me with some force. 'And now I've put my daughter and her husband at risk, too.'

'By the heavens...' Druett looked tired of the whole business, and none could have blamed him for it. 'You'd best hire not only Oldrigg, but a whole company of ruffians to guard you – or to hide you.'

'Your counsel,' I reminded him, 'was for me to go to Coke and tell him everything.'

'It was...' he yawned. 'Now I appear to be going about in circles, as do you.'

'Then get yourself home to supper,' I said. 'You've already done more than any man should... let me sit here awhile.'

A look of suspicion crossed Druett's features. 'If you're brewing some cockled scheme to free the Jessop boy, I would argue most forcefully against it,' he said.

'Go home to Frances,' I told him.

Whereupon, seeing I would brook no further discourse, he got to his feet. 'God save you, Robert,' he muttered, and went out.

I had eschewed his company, because I knew I must take this action alone. I would enlist Oldrigg, if he were willing to be a part of something done after dark, as those acts generally are that may be of questionable legality. I would return to Bedlam that evening, and use whatever means I must to have Thomas delivered into my keeping. Then I would take him to Henry Biershaw's house. After that... in truth, I had no clear notion of what would come after.

The showers had passed, and a chill wind blew as I left Westminster and rode around the city's edges to Oldrigg's lodging in Basinghall Ward, where I disrupted his supper. When I explained my purpose at the door, however, the man did not delay; indeed, he was as ready to see the matter despatched as I was. On foot, with me leading Leucippus, we passed the length of Curriers Row and left the city at Bishopsgate just as the doors were about to shut; it was curfew, and the light was fading. Then, for what I hoped would be the last time, we stood once again before Bedlam. While Oldrigg held the horse, I banged loudly upon the doors and called for a porter. I harboured hopes that it might be that lank-haired beanpole of a man, who would have been easily cowed, but it was not to be. Scantbury appeared, and at sight of Oldrigg and I, stopped inside the doorway.

'You're too late to visit,' he said. 'Our charges are being fed, and will soon be at evening prayers.'

'It's no visit,' I said, stepping closer. 'I've come to take Philip Mayne away.'

He gave a sigh, then: 'It's beyond my powers, sir, as I told you last time. He is not to be freed, and that's the end of it.'

'I had in mind a private arrangement, between you and I,' I told him, lowering my voice as befitted my role as conspirator. 'If he might be allowed to escape from the churchyard, you could be elsewhere... you saw nothing, being diverted by another of your charges. And none would know you were richer by ten crowns.'

He blinked at that: the nearest thing to sensibility I ever saw in the man. In truth I had only a little over twenty crowns in my purse, the last of the money loaned by Druett; my hope was that when it came to bargaining, it would be enough.

'That would be difficult to arrange, sir,' he said, after a pause.

'But you're the man to bring it about. I could perhaps rise to twelve crowns.'

He considered, with a glance back inside the hospital. Dim lights showed at the windows and the place was oddly quiet; then I had never been at this hour, when supper was being taken. Scantbury took a step forward, pulling the door to behind him; and my hopes rose: such a sum of money was a windfall for a man of his station.

'Did you say sixteen crowns?' he said, without expression.

'I might have said fourteen. But no more.'

Another moment passed; Oldrigg watched us, while Leucippus shifted on his hooves. Bishopsgate was closed now, the last of the city traffic gone. Curbing my impatience, I was about to urge Scantbury to an answer, when to my relief he moved close to me.

'Fifteen,' he said, and held out his hand.

'Five now,' I said, taking it. 'The remainder when Philip is delivered to me.'

He grew brisk then, as the import of our transaction was now apparent. 'Go through to the churchyard,' he said. 'The gate is fast – wait for me to unlock it.' He took the coins, and turned to go. 'And be quick, if you please.'

I waited until he had gone inside, then made haste to enter the muddy lane, which was as dark as pitch. On my instruction Oldrigg tied Leucippus to the fence, and the two of us splashed through the mire to the gate, which was locked as Scantbury had said. Here we waited, both of us growing taut when no-one came for several minutes.

'I wouldn't trust that fellow with a bent farthing, sir,' Oldrigg said. 'He's up to some mischief.'

'He won't pass up the prize of further crowns,' I said, feeling the wind about my neck. I was chilled and hungry, my feet mighty cold.

'What would you have me do, if he tries treachery?' My hired man asked. 'Though I'd like to break his fingers, it would be a matter of some risk.'

'It must not come to anything of that kind,' I answered. 'But be assured I'll reward you in any event, and say nothing of your service when we're done...'

I stopped as the rear door of the hospital opened, and a faint sound of movement followed. We could see little in the poor light, until footsteps approached and the figure of Scantbury loomed at last. Keys jangled, but instead of unlocking the gate, which was the height of my chest, he stood still.

'I fear there's some alteration, sir,' he said.

'What's that?' I demanded. 'Where's the boy?'

'Peace... he's there by the wall, but loth to come any further. I had a deal of a task to bring him outside.'

'Do you mean he refuses to come with me?' I asked – to which Scantbury's answer brought dismay.

'Well, he does not speak, as you know. The matter is, he cannot walk... or no more than a step or two, since yesternight. I fear the hunger has bested him.'

'Since last night?' I cursed aloud, but I was resolved: to be this close to a victory was more than I had expected, and nothing would prevent me now. Drawing a breath, I put my hand to the gate and shook it.

'Then undo this lock, and let us in so that we may carry him out,' I ordered.

'Well, I might do so,' Scantbury answered. 'Yet I would put myself in suspicion, having the keys... the risk, sir, now that I've weighed it, is too great. Though if you were to raise the price to eighteen crowns, perhaps-'

He was cut short. There was a flurry of movement as Oldrigg lurched past me, his hand flying out to grasp Scantbury by the arm. The man found himself jerked forwards, his arm stretched over the top of the gate. With his other hand Oldrigg drew his poniard and put it to the man's windpipe, whereupon he froze.

'Christ Jesus,' he muttered. 'I meant only to do some further wrangling...'

'Give me the keys,' I snapped, my heart thudding.

'I will,' the helpless porter said, in a tight voice. 'Better still, I'll unlock the whoreson fucking gate myself, if this man will allow me...'

'Do it.'

He did, moving only as freely as Oldrigg permitted him while keeping the blade at his throat. As soon as the padlock was sprung I pushed the gate wide, Oldrigg maintaining his grip on Scantbury's arm. Once we were through, however, he threw the man to the ground, flat on his back, and stood over him. Bending low, he held his poniard to his neck and told him not to move. Then he spoke to me, without taking his eyes off his victim.

'You'd best go and see if this one's been lying to you, sir,' he said.

There was no time to spare. Hurrying through the gathering dark, with the rear wall of the hospital at my right, I made my way to the rotted bench where Thomas and I had sat, but it was unoccupied. When I moved further towards the rear door, however, I heard sounds: raised voices from the hospital, and a shout. There was a feeble glow from a single high window, but I could see almost nothing – and for one fearful moment I feared that Scantbury had betrayed me: that Thomas was not here at all, but still inside; that the porter had meant to wring more money from me at the gate and then flee indoors – for what recourse would I have? He could deny the entire matter; worse, he could report that I'd attempted to bribe him but he'd refused. What an old fool was ex-justice Belstrang, who thought all men honoured the bargains they'd made! And more - then I tripped.

With a cry I fell over something, landing on my face in wet grass – whereupon beside me, someone whimpered like a child. Getting to my knees, I peered at a figure sitting slumped, his back against the wall beside the doorway; I had fallen over his outstretched legs. In my relief I put out a hand to grasp his shoulder – then saw his face, pale as chalk in the dim light. His eyes were closed, and he looked as near to death as to life.

'Thomas – it's Belstrang,' I said, bending over him. 'Can you hear me? Open your eyes if you can.'

Slowly, his eyes opened.

'Listen now, for I'm getting you out,' I told him, with a deal of relief. 'Can you stand? You must do your utmost, for I doubt

I can carry you... do you hear me?'

At first there was no answer; then came a hoarse whisper.

'Leave me, Master Belstrang... I beg you, let me die in this place.'

'I will not – I cannot!' I burst out – and found myself gripping his shoulders, as if to shake some spirit into him.

'I'm taking you to safety,' I told him. 'There are people who want you to live – who would help you to a confessor,' I added, somewhat desperately. 'Think – do you truly wish to be buried here, without proper ceremony? Will you not try to make your peace with God, who forgives all transgressions – and put your fate in His hands?'

Silence followed, and it was perhaps my worst moment of all. On my knees, holding him by the shoulders, I leaned close to him. 'Let me carry such tidings to your father and mother, that they may find some peace,' I implored. 'Will you not, at the least, do that? For their sake – and for mine?'

I was close to shedding tears. To be thwarted at this final pass, knowing it was the last chance this wretched boy would have, was not to be borne. In anguish I threw a glance over my shoulder, to where I supposed Oldrigg still kept guard over Scantbury; hearing no sound, I turned back to Thomas - and at last, came what many would call an answer to a prayer.

'I will try to get up,' he said, in little more than a whisper.

I let out a long breath, and got clumsily to my feet. Reaching down, I took Thomas by his upper arm, feeling the stick-thin limb through his rough coat. But when I attempted to raise him, I was undone: he put his other hand to the ground and tried to lift himself, but fell back.

'Your pardon,' he breathed. 'I cannot.'

I cursed, and tried to lift him by my own strength, but to no avail: though he weighed little after months of fasting, it was too much for me. But I had hope now: no longer was he resisting, but had shown willingness. Hence there was only one course open: I would have to drag him.

'Pardon me, Thomas,' I said, to which he made no response, even when I seized his arm and pulled him away bodily from the wall. I took a breath, put my hands under his armpits and heaved, and mercifully we began to move. Backwards through the churchyard I drew him, catching my feet at times, past the bench again, until I thought myself far enough from the hospital door to risk calling out. Somewhat breathlessly I hailed Oldrigg, and received a reply.

''I have him,' I puffed. 'Leave the porter, for you must help me. I can't go much further alone…'

I flinched as, without warning, Oldrigg appeared at my side. Now I feared that Scantbury would cry out, or run – until my soldier-servant allayed my fears.

'There's no call to fret about him, sir,' he said, with a calmness that shamed me. 'He's trussed like a fowl - bound with his own belt and sleeves, his mouth stopped with his stinking hose. I'll leave him like that, if you wish. But for now, if you'll stand aside, I mean to throw your friend over my shoulder and take him out up the lane. Leucippus can do the rest – are you content?'

'I'm content,' I said, breathing hoarsely. 'In truth, I believe I'm the most contented man you could find just now - even here, among the dead.'

SIXTEEN

We reached Henry Biershaw's house an hour later, having travelled through Moorfields and around the outside of the city walls, to enter Shoe Lane from Holborn Hill. The journey was made in silence, after we set our backs to Bedlam and made haste to get clear. Scantbury, somewhat against Oldrigg's will, had been freed from his bonds and paid off in full, hence I expected no further difficulties from him; perhaps my relief at having brought Thomas away imbued me with a surfeit of satisfaction.

Thomas was on Leucippus, a limp and pitiful sight who at times had to be supported by Oldrigg while I led the horse. Night was upon us, and I was glad to come at last to the house of the glass-painter, though I was unsure how he would receive us. And when he opened the door with a lantern, alarmed by my knocking, he was shocked by what he saw.

'You may find it hard to recognise him at first, Master Biershaw,' I said, 'but I assure you it's the one you know as Philip.'

He blinked hard at the emaciated figure, who was being held on his feet by Oldrigg. 'By the good lord,' he murmured, 'what's been done to him?'

Without waiting for answer, he turned and led the way inside. And so at last, with some difficulty, Thomas Jessop was brought to the Biershaws' fireside where he sat shivering, his threadbare clothing having been no protection against the night air. Finding himself surrounded by people he flinched, until he recognised the faces of his hosts, who regarded him with dismay.

'He must be washed and put to bed, once he's warmed himself,' Catherine Biershaw said firmly. 'Do you know us, Philip?' she asked him.

'I do, Mistress Catherine,' came the answer, in a hoarse whisper. 'I'm most glad to see you...' his eyes went to her husband. 'Is that Henry?'

'We're all here, boy,' Biershaw said in a subdued voice. As if to confirm his words Colley came in then, filling the room with his bulk – and at sight of the figure seated by the fire, he gave a cry.

'What's become of Philip?' he demanded, bringing his hands together and working them nervously. 'Who has hurt him?'

'He's sick, Colley,' Catherine Biershaw said at once. 'But now that he's here we may help him get well again. Until he's ready to be on his way, that is.'

She caught my eye, and I understood: I had brought danger to her home. With a nod to her, I went outside with Oldrigg to the street door. My concern was for Leucippus, who needed feed and rest; if I was willing, Oldrigg said, he would take him to the stable by St Bride's. I pressed coins into his hand and thanked him with all my heart, whereupon he inclined his head.

'Had I not known otherwise, sir, I would never have taken you for a Justice,' he said. 'You are a most curious man.'

'You're a most incurious man,' I told him. 'And I wish I could reward you better for your service. I can but wish you well from this day forth.'

He attempted a smile, which suited him not at all, and we parted. I closed the door upon him and returned to the Biershaws, where I came upon an unexpected sight: Colley seated on the floor beside Thomas, rubbing his feet and hands to warm them and murmuring softly, as if to a pet dog. Catherine was gone to heat some broth, Biershaw told me, and if I wished to speak further we might go to his workshop. I followed him to the rear of the house, into the darkened room where he brought his lantern and set it on the bench.

'My wife is most uneasy,' Biershaw said. 'As are we all… and I would like to have some words of assurance from you, that we're not greatly endangered by having Philip under our roof.'

'I would like nothing more than to give you those words, Master Biershaw,' I replied. 'But in truth I cannot.'

He regarded me in silence.

'I can but make a promise,' I went on. 'That if you let him rest here for a few nights and take some nourishment, I'll return as soon as I've made my preparations to return him to his father's house. And if any man comes to you with questions, you may tell him it was at my behest that you gave him shelter. You need say no more than that.'

'You ask me to lie, then?' The glass-painter said.

'I do not,' I told him. 'You have committed no crime, you merely gave succour to a poor soul in need. How he was brought here is not your concern.'

'What meaning must I take from that, sir?' Biershaw asked. 'That he escaped from Bedlam, and you helped him?'

'And if I did so,' I said after a moment, 'would you condemn me for it?'

He looked away then. 'No man would, who had an ounce of Christian charity,' he answered. 'Yet you know our condition, and how close we are to penury. I could not pay a fine, and we have Colley to look out for.'

'I know it.' With a sigh I glanced about the room, and my eye fell on the armorial window pane, now almost complete. In the warm light of the lantern, it seemed to glow of its own accord.

'I wish I had the means to order a set of such glasses from you, to adorn my old house,' I said, with admiration. 'My father would have delighted to see our crest emblazoned so finely.'

Biershaw did not answer - whereupon as I turned to him, a sudden dizziness came upon me, so that I almost staggered. I had eaten nothing since noon, and the day had been one of turmoil, the like of which I had not undergone since being imprisoned in the Compter. I put a hand to my head, whereupon at once the glass-painter reached out to steady me.

'You'd best rest yourself here for the night, Master Belstrang,' he said, looking me over keenly. 'I've slept in the workshop myself, at times. If you'll sit a while, I'll make up a pallet.'

He moved to the door, and I sank down on the stool before his work-bench. Just then, a pallet on the floor was as welcome as a feather bed.

In the morning I took farewell of my hosts, with gratitude for their kindnesses. I had slept like a dead man, helped by a posset brought to the workshop by Mistress Biershaw. I shared breakfast with them, of porridge and hard bread, after which I paid Biershaw all that I could spare. Thomas was asleep in the room he had once occupied as a lodger. Colley sat beside his bed, Catherine said, and was content to watch over him; never had she seen him so tender and attentive towards anyone. He could be a healer, perhaps... a notion that gave her hope. Though Philip was as weak as a kitten, she thought: the unspoken fact between us being that he was in no fit condition to travel any distance. Though this troubled me, I had to set it aside: the pressing business of having to accompany George to Westminster was uppermost in my thoughts.

I left in some haste, to retrieve Leucippus from the stable and see that he had been fed. That done, in the grey morning with the city suburbs busy, I got myself mounted and rode northwards again towards Highgate. As I rode, thoughts flew about my mind unchecked; the rescue of Thomas, as I saw it, being just one of the dangers I had brought upon myself. In truth I had only one desire now, which was to extricate both him and myself by some means and journey homewards. The difficulty was that the youth I had spent such energies trying to free was now, given his condition, the main obstacle to my leaving. *Now bind my brows with irony...* I parodied the poet with bitter humour, putting a *y* to his last word.

My bones ached as I rode, not least my legs; Childers would have berated me for misusing my body so, not least because for him the whole mission had been futile from the outset, if not plain wrong. But Hester would understand; I missed her calmness and her compassion. Spring was arriving, despite the day's chill, and the cherry-trees would be in flower at Thirldon; I had not missed the Easter festivities in more than twenty years. And the King, Druett had said, would return soon from his hunting...

On a sudden, I was gripping the rein tightly, my hands stiff inside my gloves. I had no appetite for another visit to Westminster, which to my mind seemed to resemble a malodorous beehive, though one without harmony or purpose. What benefit might come from George and I taking our testimony to Sir Edward Coke, I could not anticipate: precious little, I feared, not sharing George's trust in the Chief Justice – nor Druett's hopes of his mercy. The tangled business of the projected plot that had driven Thomas Jessop into madness, and seemingly ended at least one life –that of Anstis – was the stuff of nightmares. And yet, I wondered, since at the final turn no attempted regicide had ever taken place, and those who knew of the scheme were few in number, who would believe it? Moreover, who among the King's councillors, servants and protectors would admit they had been remiss enough to allow it to grow? Would not their first intent be to guard themselves against censure – to dismiss the whole matter, and brand it a mere fancy?

But what weighed most heavily on my mind was the fate of Thomas; once the tale was told, he would likely be arrested immediately. Hence, as I rode, a somewhat desperate notion came to me: to persuade George to keep the misguided dupe's true name a secret. I had small hope of succeeding, but I would try. The thought was still fresh when I arrived at the house to find him already outside, with his horse saddled and waiting… and one look at his face was enough to dampen any man's spirits.

'You are muddied and tousled, sir,' he said, with a disapproving look. 'It would be unseemly to seek an audience with Sir Edward, looking as you do.'

'Perhaps I should forgo that pleasure, then,' I said, with coolness.

'I do not think it a matter for jest,' he replied. 'Will you come inside and clean yourself? I will provide you with fresh linen.'

I dismounted and went indoors, leaving George to follow. And there was Anne, her face filled with concern at sight of me. But when she began to ask questions, I stayed her.

'I'll not speak of it now,' I told her. 'Where is my beautiful granddaughter? I would embrace her, save that I'm in need of washing.'

'Well then, you'd best see to it,' she said, somewhat briskly.

The business was completed in a short time. In an upstairs room I disrobed, and George's manservant took my clothes and boots to be brushed and made clean. Warm water and cloths appeared, by which I was able to restore myself to some semblance of dignity after the previous night's venture. In borrowed shirt and hose, I clad myself again and descended to find George pacing the main room, hat in hand and eager to be gone. It struck me that, despite what had passed between us the day before, he was as nervous of an audience with the Chief Justice as was I. Hence, for better or for worse, I decided to tell him what had been done: that I had removed Thomas Jessop from Bedlam.

'And may I ask where you've taken him?' He asked, after a moment.

'You may, but I would prefer not to tell you just now,' I said. 'Moreover,' I added, 'I have a request to make, which is most important to me.'

'What that might be, pray?'

'That in recounting the conspiracy before Coke, neither of us speaks the real name of the plotters' instrument – the one who was to take the blame for their design. I ask that you refer to him by the name he is known here: Philip Mayne.'

George frowned, and I knew what his answer would be – how could I have expected otherwise? He considered for a moment, then:

'Have you forgotten that, from what you told me, Edmund Anstis knew who he was and whence he came?' he demanded. 'Hence it would be utter foolishness to pretend otherwise. Even,' he added with a dour look, 'were I willing to do so.'

'But Anstis is dead,' I answered, 'and it's possible he never told anyone Thomas's true name – he was to be known as Mayne from the moment he reached London. All I ask is that you call him such, as will I.'

'So, you want me to lie,' George said.

'I want you to help me save that wretched young man's life.'

He looked away. And though I was eager to press him, seeing his expression I held my tongue – and was surprised by what followed.

'You and your daughter are... you are so alike,' he murmured.

I waited, until he faced and said: 'She has spent a good portion of last night endeavouring to persuade me to the very same action. I refused her.'

I met his gaze. 'And are you still of the same mind?' I asked.

'I was, until you came. Now, you tell me you have effected a rescue – or a kidnap, as some might call it. Hence, I am even more inclined to stay firm…'

On a sudden, he grew impatient again. 'But see, it's likely of no consequence – it's for others to decide how to proceed. I'll waste no more time. Will you take a drink before we leave, or no?'

I declined. My hopes were dashed, but there seemed no remedy, and now I was as eager to have done with the business as he was. When Anne appeared, holding Kate by the hand, I took a brief moment to greet my granddaughter and to beg her pardon for having brought no gift for her. I would repair that soon, I promised, but just now I was called away. Whereupon with few words, and a heavy heart again, I took my leave of them both and left the house.

We rode in silence, from Highgate down through Kentish Town, then by Pancras and Totten Court to Westminster. It was a curious journey: two lawyers, kinsmen by marriage but of such different minds, bound by a fearful secret. Despite my years, I felt at times as though George were the master and I a recalcitrant pupil, destined for punishment. And yet the ride afforded me an opportunity to think, and to ready myself for what would doubtless be stern questioning. By the time we came to the bustling village of Whitehall Palace and its environs, I had rehearsed some justification for my actions; or so I thought, until the reality of our arrival threw the matter into another light. In short, after stabling the horses and proceeding on foot to the Chief Justice's rooms, we were thwarted before we had begun.

'What can you mean, you must deny me access?' George demanded of the ferret-faced clerk who barred our way. 'I'm an advocate, formerly of the Temple. I have important tidings for your master, which touch on matters of state. It's imperative that I see him at once.'

'Sir Edward is fully engaged, sir,' the clerk said. 'You will understand that matters of state take precedence over all else. You may submit a petition in writing, or join others who wait elsewhere.' His eyes wandered towards me and back to George, who was puffing himself up in his familiar manner.

'I dare not and will not commit the matter to paper,' he said sharply. 'I speak of...' He stopped himself; I believe he was about to mouth the word *treason*, but thought better of it. The clerk then saw fit to ask our names, which were given; by which time a feeling of deep unease had stolen over me.

'Perhaps we should return another time,' I ventured to say.

'And be refused again?' George snapped. 'It cannot wait,' he said to the clerk. 'Believe me when I say that, once Sir Edward hears me out, he will be convinced of the gravity of the matter. You do yourself no good by preventing me.'

'Your pardon, sir, but I have my instructions,' the clerk insisted. 'You really cannot come to the Chief Justice at your pleasure, as if he were a mere lawyer like yourself, ready to hear from some plaintiff or other. If you go too far in this, you will oblige me to call for men-at-arms to escort you out.'

'That will not be necessary,' I said. I plucked at George's sleeve, but angrily he pulled it away.

'I know full well you're eager to be gone,' he said, aside to me. 'Yet the matter cannot rest – you know it yourself.'

We were distracted then, as without warning the clerk turned away, opened the door to which he had forbidden us access, and poked his head within. There was an exchange of words, which we could not hear, before the man faced us again, pulling the door closed.

'If you'd care to wait a while, sirs, there is one who might aid you,' he said, with a slight frown. 'Will you walk out to the yard? Someone will come presently.'

For a moment I thought George would offer further resistance, but he agreed. The two of us walked out to New Palace Yard, where we stood by the fountain as I had done but three days before. In the breeze that blew across from Lambeth we waited in silence, looking out at the river traffic. George was barely able to master his nervousness, I saw, being so occupied with the business that he could not rest until he had unburdened himself of it. Odd, I thought fleetingly, that it was I who had once been censured for my impatience by my puritan son-in-law; and indeed, I sensed that George himself felt he had lost some standing in my eyes. Whatever the case, he refused to look at me until, when our wait had grown tedious, a different servant appeared, made his bow and asked us to follow him.

We did so, George striding ahead, a gloom-faced Robert Belstrang behind, into another part of the palace. Past armed guards we walked, down dim corridors, until finally we fetched up at another door. Bidding us wait, the servant knocked and went inside, then reappeared at once and stood holding the door wide. As we entered the room, where a good sea-coal fire burned, a well-dressed courtier, grey-haired and grey-bearded, rose from a table covered with a rich Turkey carpet. And at sight of him, George stopped in his tracks.

'Sir Roland…?'

'Machyn,' the courtier finished. 'And you're Bull. While you, sir…' He shifted his gaze to me. 'Your face is unfamiliar, but perhaps your name will be less so.'

I gave it, with a perfunctory nod. Sir Roland Machyn… I raked my memory for particulars of the man, but could find nothing. Though from his manner and dress it was clear he was an official of some standing, he was not one of the Council. Yet it was all one now, I thought, for we were come to it at last: the laying forth of the whole fearful business of the Anniversary Plot. And though the feeling of unease had not left me, not since the Chief Justice's clerk had asked my name, I managed to look composed. That is, until Machyn's next words proved disconcerting.

'Of course.' He levelled a pair of hawkish eyes at me. 'Robert Belstrang, whose reputation precedes him. Who traded insults with a servant of one of the Secretaries of State, later drowned. Who has consorted with Papists of a troublesome nature, seemingly indifferent to any resultant damage to his reputation. Who now comes to the seat of government again, almost as if he were an entitled fellow, instead of a former Justice from the shires who lost his place, I seem to recall. And who now stands like a penitent, ripe for confession. Perhaps we should find you a priest – would that please you?'

Well – I freely admit I was both abashed and insulted. In my youth I might have challenged him to withdraw his hard words or face me at single combat, but those times were long past. It was a pretty enough speech, I had to admit, intended to instil fear in me as Anstis had tried to do a week ago. But this time I was caught: George could not help me, nor Druett, nor anyone else. There was no course open except to give a full account of all that I knew, and put myself at this man's mercy. And as if to show that he had as good as read my thoughts Machyn nodded, and a dry smile appeared.

'No priest, then,' he murmured. 'Very well, you must make do with me. And so, Master Bull...' he looked to George, raising his eyebrows. 'Would you like to give me these important tidings, touching on matters of state, which you were so eager to impart to the Chief Justice? I'm willing to listen.'

'I will,' George said quickly; he was more chastened than I had ever seen him. 'And if you please, my father-in-law is here to give his testimony, as he has already told it to me. I regret it will take some time...'

He swallowed and looked about the room, whereupon Machyn's smile broadened. Deliberately, he sat down behind his richly-caparisoned table and settled himself comfortably.

'I regret there are neither chairs nor stools for you, sirs,' he said. 'Now – shall we begin?'

SEVENTEEN

Sir Roland Machyn, I might say, is someone I have often thought of since that day at Whitehall. He was shrewd, and from his manner a *skeptic*, in the spirit of those ancients I admire. He appeared not as a man who would rush to judgement, but one who notes every part of a subject, favouring none. In silence he listened as George, his words spilling out in haste, relayed the bare details of the intended attempt upon the King's life. And to my surprise and relief, George referred to the would-be assassin throughout as Philip Mayne.

I was confounded: what, I wondered, had brought about this change of heart? Thought it became clear to me that giving testimony before this man, whose name he appeared to know, caused George considerable strain. After a while he ran out of breath, or out of courage, and invited me to speak. I did so truthfully, though omitting Jane Rudlin's name: I would not involve her further. Of course, I did not speak of my activities of the previous day either; and to my further relief George had made no mention of Philip Mayne's being freed from Bedlam. When I was done, I invited Machyn to put me under oath and let me swear to the veracity of my testimony; the suggestion, however, was ignored.

'Most wonderful,' he said, after a pause. 'Master Jonson, or perhaps Master Fletcher, could make a comedy of it.'

In some confusion, we waited.

'A comedy of gossip and hearsay, with a chorus of Bedlam fools to please the mob,' Machyn went on. 'I've not heard the like in years. And the late Edmund Anstis, a loyal servant to the Crown, was the instigator of this plot, you say? How unfortunate that he's no longer able to confess to it, or to deny it.'

There was a tightness in my stomach. Machyn was not merely toying with us, I sensed: there was an undertone of malice. From the corner of my eye I saw George standing stiff and upright, stilled by his words.

'I do not say he was the only instigator,' I ventured. 'But from what I have learned, and from his behaviour towards me, I'm certain he was a part of it.'

'As certain as you can be.'

'There is little doubt in my mind.'

'What of you, Bull?' He swung his gaze towards George. 'Is there doubt in your mind?' And when George hesitated: 'Come, there's no profit in holding back now. As a man of legal training, you would not seek an audience with the Chief Justice on a mere whim. Does your father-in-law's testimony not hold firm?'

'I believe it does, sir,' George managed to say. 'As I know him to be a man of honour.'

A silence followed in which Machyn shifted his gaze between us. Then, to our discomfort, he gave a shout of laughter.

'Well, what a tale you've spun,' he said, with a shake of his head. 'It would be laughed at in any court in England. Yet I see you are in earnest, hence I must question your motives in bringing it here. What reward did you hope to gain by it?'

'Reward, sir?' George was stung. 'I harboured no such thought – merely a desire to see a nest of Popish plotters uncovered and brought to book. The King's life was in danger – it's a matter of treason.'

'Indeed?' Machyn regarded him as he might have done a student who had made a poor stab at argument. 'And had it not occurred to you that the whole thing could have been concocted by this feeble-minded papist from the shires – this Mayne? He would not be the first to go ranting about London, spreading lies and fancies. There's one man who claims he's the son of the late Queen Elizabeth by the Earl of Essex, and demands his right to the crown... who can fathom such madness?'

I glanced at George, and saw that he was dismayed. Having come to Whitehall with good intentions, as he believed, to be rebuffed and humiliated in this manner was intolerable to him. He was forming a reply, but Machyn stayed him.

'Let me be charitable, and take it your purpose is honourable,' he said, in a more conciliatory tone. 'But you must know there are always plot rumours circulating, which turn out to be without substance. What evidence do you have, aside from hearsay, to set this one apart from the rest? The man you say was the prime mover, or one of them, is dead - by his own hand, some say. He had numerous debts, and no shortage of enemies – but he was no papist. While your other witness is a madman confined in Bedlam…' He put on a pitying smile. 'What did you think – that the Council would set aside all other business, and fall to investigating this mess of wild accusations?'

'I thought it my duty,' George answered, controlling himself with difficulty. 'As I believe it is the duty of every loyal Englishman to be vigilant in these times.'

'Most laudable,' Machyn said, with sarcasm. In apparent unconcern, he sat back in his chair and turned his gaze upon me. 'Yet your presence, Belstrang, troubles me rather more,' he continued. 'Perhaps you'd care to tell me why you quarrelled with Anstis, not long before he died. From what I hear swords were drawn - which is a grave matter in this place, even when the King is absent.'

'The only sword drawn was that of Anstis, sir,' I answered. 'He took exception to my telling him what I'd learned about him – as I took exception to him having me clapped in the Counter for a debt that never existed. I've told you what I believe: that it was he who picked Mayne out for this stratagem -'

'You have,' Machyn broke in. 'And as I've said it's most unfortunate – if not convenient – that the man can no longer substantiate your tale.'

In truth, by this time I was struggling to contain myself. The man's scornful tone, his ridiculing of both George and myself, coupled with his dismissal of the testimony I had agonised over giving, was becoming too much to bear – and hence, I spoke words which I immediately regretted.

'Perhaps Antis's master, Sir Thomas Lake, would wish to hear the entire tale, as you call it,' I said. 'No doubt his undersecretary's actions would reflect badly upon him, and for that reason alone he would doubtless want the matter laid open, so that it can be investigated in a proper manner.'

There was a short silence, in which I heard George draw a sharp breath. It was rash of me, of course, to speak in that manner to a man like Machyn. He, however, showed neither surprise nor concern.

'Well then,' he said, 'perhaps you should put the entire business in writing. I'll see that Sir Thomas receives it, when he returns from Royston with His Majesty.'

At that, I berated myself inwardly. Were George or I to do what he suggested, I realised, there was no certainty that Sir Thomas Lake or anyone else would see the document - might it even go straight on the fire? For in truth, nobody in the royal circle would wish to tell King James of yet another suspected plot, when the very thought of such, I had heard, would cause the man to quail in terror. The doubts I'd had during my ride to Highgate that morning returned - that the King's servants' chief concerns would be for their own protection: to dismiss the story, and so deflect any blame that might be directed at them. Now I understood Machyn's purpose - which to my shame, afforded me enormous relief. For he was offering us an egress: to leave the whole troublesome topic behind and, having done what we thought was right, go about our lives in peace... at which moment the man spoke up again, with unconcealed menace.

'I will say a little more,' he said, sitting upright on a sudden. 'You have brought the matter here, with what I will choose to regard as good intentions. You may set it down as a report if you wish, by which action you will have proved faithful to your account, which would then receive due attention. Should you be required to give further testimony, you may be summoned.'

He stopped. There was a threat coming; I could feel it. Beside me, George swallowed audibly.

'However...' Machyn eyed each of us in turn. 'Should you spread further rumours - wholly unsubstantiated rumours, I would add - of this supposed plot, you run a most serious risk of arrest. For there are other forms of treason: Sir Edward Coke has written of them himself. As men of the law, you will be familiar with the quotation: "Diverse Acts of Parliament have ordained that compassing by bare words or sayings should be high treason." And though he goes on to say that bare words may make a heretic, but not a traitor, there is a further sentence to the effect that, "if the same be set down in writing by the delinquent himself, this is a sufficient overt act within this statute".'

'But sir – that is a distortion!'

George was aghast. 'It's not the one who reports the treason who condemns himself,' he said quickly, 'but the one who intended it - you pick phrases at haphazard. Hence, I consider-'

'You consider what?' Machyn stopped him in mid flow. 'Do you presume to instruct me on a point of law?'

'No, and yet I cannot… or, I would not wish…'

Poor George: his words tumbled over themselves, but I was ready to come to his aid, for it was time to bring this interlude to a close. There was a door half-open, as there had been a real door ajar that time in Anstis's room - and I did not intend to forgo the chance of passing through it.

'We understand perfectly, sir,' I said to Machyn, signalling with a glance at George that he should close his mouth. 'As lawyers, we thought it right to appraise the Chief Justice of the matter as we saw it, in confidence, and let him act as he thought fit. I will swear I had no thought of reward, nor did my son-in-law Master Bull, who is a man of good standing. You have heard us in full, and will no doubt decide what action to take.'

'Rest assured that I will,' Machyn said, after a moment; he was regarding me intently, as if unsure whether or not to believe me. 'But for the present, you have entertained me long enough.'

And with that, it was finished.

I made a brief bow, George followed suit, and in silence we got ourselves outside. As I went, I took a last look at Sir Roland Machyn and found his gaze upon me. There was no mistaking his warning: the Anniversary Plot had never existed - and I would pursue all mention of it at my peril.

Outside, in the cool air, we walked for some distance without speaking. Finally George stopped and turned to me; never had I seen him so shaken.

'I should beg your pardon,' he said. 'For insisting upon this…' he shook his head. 'For bringing about that shameful interlude.'

'You know him, this Machyn,' I said, surprised by his humility.

'By sight, and by reputation. He serves the senior Secretary of State – Sir Ralph Winwood himself.'

'Not a man you would want to offend, then,' I said, as the words sank in.

He looked sharply at me, but there was no rebuke. For perhaps the first time in our relations, George and I shared a close and private understanding: we had been warned off, in no uncertain fashion. Henceforth we should avoid all talk of this plot, as if it had been but a chimera from the start. However, while my own dismay at the planned regicide had by now evaporated in my concern to get Thomas away, George's outrage had been quelled by the threat of consequences. In short, a man in his position had too much to lose.

'You should go to your family now, and comfort them,' I said.

'And henceforth, observe my best behaviour,' he replied, with an edge of bitterness. 'Like a schoolboy who's been caned, and durst not transgress again.'

'If you mean to continue in the law, and to advance yourself – then yes.'

We began to walk again, proceeding to the palace stables to retrieve our mounts. I led Leucippus out into the yard and waited for George to follow. At sight of his dejected countenance, I was moved to pity him.

'You're a man of high ideals, George Bull,' I said. 'A little too high for me, at times. But you yourself spoke of how much England has changed. Men like Machyn know the field, where it's safe to tread and where not. In truth, you shame me with your striving to act rightly, despite your feelings towards the King and his Council. But you have been brought to a barrier, one that's beyond your skill or mine to surmount.'

He stood beside his horse, one hand on its mane. 'Yet it will forever be in my mind,' he said. 'It irks me greatly when the guilty go unpunished. We're all sinners, and only God can choose who is saved and who is damned - yet we must strive. Otherwise, what are we but beasts of the forest?'

'Well, I tend towards the wisdom of the ancients, those whom you regard as pagan,' I told him. 'Men are ever as the times are. And there are few things of certainty, save the passing of time – and the need to move with it, or be thrown aside.'

'You mean bend to the tide, and to the devil with my piety,' he answered.

'Go on home,' I said again. 'I'll return to your house, before I leave London.'

And we parted before the Temple Bars, close to the law schools where we had both studied: George to ride north to Highgate, I eastwards along Fleet Street and thence through the city, to Coleman Street and Druett's.

A weight was lifted from me, and I could not help but be mighty glad of its passing. I would write to Hester telling her that I would return within the week, as I felt certain of doing. I was weary of London: its reek, its noise and bustle – its harshness. I rode past the Bel Savage and was reminded of all that had occurred there, before thinking again of Thomas Jessop, who I hoped was recovering some of his strength. There were preparations to make, after I had spoken with Druett again; I would make out a letter of promise for the money I owed him, and repay him as soon as I was home. Having things to occupy me lifted my spirits, so that I even dropped a penny in a beggar's bowl at Ludgate. Thereafter I picked my way through the crowded streets, thinking of home.

At Druett's house all was tranquillity, which was balm to me after those hours of turmoil. I took dinner with Frances, who to my relief asked no questions about my activities the previous night. I wrote a short letter to Hester, reassuring her that all was well, and paid a boy to take it for despatch. And yet I found myself restless thereafter, my eagerness to take Thomas Jessop home tempered by a feeling of dissatisfaction at the way matters had fallen out. When Druett returned in the late afternoon we talked in his private closet, surrounded by books and documents, the trappings of the lawyer. Though I was unsure how he would receive the news, I believed he deserved a full account of my actions at Bedlam and the appearance before Sir

Roland Machyn... but when I was done, he was close to dismay.

'There's little doubt in my mind about one thing, Robert,' he said. 'Your son-in-law Bull is a fool.'

'Naïve, perhaps, and a precisian who maddens me at times,' I answered. 'But he believed he was acting from loyalty, and meant to put everything before Coke. He did not expect to face Machyn, who daunted him somewhat.'

'He daunts most men,' Druett said. 'He's been close to Sir Ralph Winwood ever since Winwood was ambassador in The Hague. Now he's the Secretary's eyes and ears – they say he has his own little nest of spies. Once again, you've run a considerable risk.' He frowned, then: 'As for threatening to lay the matter before Lake - Winwood's bitter rival – that was rashness personified.'

'I should have curbed my indignation,' I admitted. 'But the man treated us with disdain in his eagerness to have the whole tale, as he called it, laid to rest. If I weren't glad to leave the matter, now that Thomas is freed, I could almost be tempted to pen a report and send it to Lake anonymously, merely to discomfort Machyn and his ilk.'

At that my friend grew impatient. 'That was a most reckless thing you did – I mean bribing a porter to let Jessop out of Bedlam. How do you know the man won't talk to save his own skin, once the absence is noted? Moreover, how do you know you can trust Oldrigg, who merely works for hire like any mercenary soldier? You've allowed yourself to become too embroiled in this business, far beyond a mere favour to a neighbour. Can you be certain of getting the man's wretched son home without further difficulties? Moreover, writing to Lake – even anonymously -would be the height of folly.'

'I said I could almost be tempted,' I said, somewhat lamely. 'I've no wish to draw more fire from any quarter.'

'But don't you see, you have done so already?'

Druett's tone was sharp. And when I had no ready answer, he went on: 'Do you believe Machyn will simply let the matter drop, as he told you to do under threat? You may be certain he'll take it straight to his master, Winwood, as soon as he can. He would be a fool not to, lest it spill from some other source and it emerged he knew of it. And whatever else he is, the man's no fool. I've said it before: Whitehall's a teeming morass - every man striving to outwit and to outrun his fellows, no matter who gets trampled.'

He paused a moment, then: 'I'm uncertain how to counsel you, Robert. Some might advise you to tie Thomas Jessop onto a horse, get him out of the suburbs without delay and pay someone else to take him home. Then you can build some testimony to establish your innocence – write it, and swear to it on oath.'

'Some might advise it, but not you?' I enquired.

'I?' He let out a sigh. 'I'm at a loss. And should you ask me to be your witness to such an oath, I'm uncertain as to whether I could.'

'I would never ask it,' I said at once. 'You've done more than any man would...' and as the thought occurred: 'I should go to the Biershaws now, before evening comes, and see how Thomas fares. Though I fear a journey of two days, or perhaps three, may be a sore trial to him.'

I rose, for there was little more to discuss. In truth, after what Druett had said my relief of the morning had given way to more foreboding. I had already stretched our friendship, I knew, and I should prepare for departure with whatever haste I could. I made ready to ride and left the city by Cripplegate, passing round the walls to Holborn and thence to Shoe Lane once more. Arriving at Henry Biershaw's door, however, I found the house dark, the windows covered.

I dismounted, allowing Leucippus's rein to trail on the ground, and knocked on the door. There was no answer, and I was reminded of my first visit, when there had been a delay before Biershaw appeared, blinking in that owlish way of his. I knocked again, more loudly, to no avail, then with impatience rapped on the window with my knuckles. But nobody came.

I paused and looked about: there were few people in the street, and none nearby. Putting my ear to the door, I believed I heard sounds. Perhaps the family were in fear of visitors, I reasoned, in view of the person they now housed under their roof. Knowing I would not be satisfied until I had seen Thomas and been assured of his safety, I banged on the door again, hard enough to set its timbers trembling, whereupon at last there came a sound. It was not the door which opened, however, but the window, with a creak of shutters and the squeal of a seldom-used latch. And there was the face of Catherine Biershaw, peering at me from within. At sight of me, she drew back.

'I'll not open my door to you again, sir,' she said. 'I won't, and there's naught you can say to persuade me.'

'Why so?' I demanded. 'What in heaven's name is the matter?'

'You know well enough,' came her tart reply. 'Our family's been turned upside down ever since you came here – and now we're done with you.'

'Mistress Biershaw... Catherine...' I leaned forward so that my head was almost inside the window. 'Has something occurred? If so, please tell me-'

'You know what's occurred,' she threw back. 'You sent your man today - that ruffian who carried Philip in here. He was hard and cruel to Henry, and now that Philip's gone Colley is beside himself. It was all your doing, and you'd best go because there's nothing for you here.'

'Wait... I don't understand,' I said in consternation. 'I never sent any man here...' then, as her words struck home: 'What - are you saying to me that Oldrigg came and took Philip away?'

'You know full well he did,' Catherine Biershaw retorted, 'for it was on your orders. He said it wasn't safe, and you'd told him to do it. I wish we'd never taken Philip in as we did – you misused Henry, with his soft heart. Now Philip's gone and that's the end of it, so please let us alone!'

She closed the window, with a bang that startled Leucippus. I went to his side to soothe him, the woman's angry words still ringing in my head. I heard them again, in confusion and in dismay: Oldrigg had returned to the Biershaws, claiming it was by my order, and taken Thomas.

As to why he would do so, it was a profound and utter mystery.

EIGHTEEN

Riding back into the city as evening drew in, I was in turmoil once again. It was as grave a matter as I had yet faced; I knew not what to think, nor whom to trust – could I even be sure of Druett now? I had little choice, however, but to take Leucippus back to the house and leave him in the stable. Without going indoors, I then set off at once to walk the short distance to Basinghall Street and the house where Oldrigg lodged. Given what had occurred I was doubtful of finding him, but there was no other place where I might begin to discover why he had done this thing. As for whose orders he was acting upon – for I could not believe he would take such action alone – that too puzzled and alarmed me greatly.

I reached the house in minutes, and with some relief saw a glow of firelight from within. I knocked and waited, hand on sword, ready to use what authority I had to question Oldrigg's landlord, whom I had never seen. I knew his name - John Baggot – but nothing more; and when the door opened at last I was surprised by the sight of a very old, stooped man, bald save for a few white hairs on his liver-spotted scalp, who peered at me with unveiled suspicion.

'Master Baggot?' I asked. 'I'm seeking your lodger, Oldrigg. Is he here?'

'He is not.' The voice was as cracked as a raven's. 'Nor am I the Baggot you want. That's my son, who isn't here either.'

'Your son is John Baggot?'

'He is…' the old man's brow furrowed. 'What has he done?'

'Nothing, that I know of,' I said. 'It's Oldrigg I want to see – have you any notion where he might be?'

'I do not,' came the reply. 'John might know… I expect him after sunset. You can return then, if you choose.' And he would have closed the door upon me, had I not prevented him.

'I do not choose it,' I said, using my Justice voice. 'It's a matter of urgency – may I come inside and wait?'

There was a pause as the older Baggot looked me over, noting my manner of dress and my sword. But he appeared unconcerned, and I sensed a strength that belied his frail appearance. Eventually he gave a sigh, and said: 'It's not a matter of arrest, is it? For Oldrigg, I mean – do you hold a warrant?'

'Why, do you think that likely?' I asked.

'Likely?' He sniffed. 'It's but a matter of time, I'd say.' Whereupon he turned to go, but left the door ajar. I followed him as he shuffled inside, and closed the door against the evening chill. I found myself in a comfortable enough room with a well-banked fire, beside which the old man sank down on a padded stool. Seeing him disinclined to speak further, I sat facing him.

'Until a short while ago, Oldrigg was serving me,' I said. 'I would be glad to hear what you know of him – in particular, why you thought he might be arrested.'

'Because men like him don't change,' he said, without looking at me. 'What do you want with him?'

I would not speak of that, I told him. Instead I asked him how Oldrigg came to be living here. Were he and the younger Baggot friends... comrades-in-arms, perhaps? Unexpectedly, he gave a bitter laugh.

'They both fought, across the sea, if that's what you mean,' he said. 'You'd best ask John... I'm no better than a lodger here myself.'

He lapsed into silence, staring at the fire. I sensed that I would get nothing further from him, and after a while I stood up, being too restless to stay seated. Here was more cloudy business, I thought; and soon I was chiding myself for my haste in hiring Oldrigg that day, on recommendation from people I did not know. Thinking upon the man's behaviour since, not least his readiness to use violent means, I grew anxious with thoughts of what he had done with Thomas Jessop, and on whose instruction. Was it Machyn who had ordered the abduction, within a short time of our meeting? Had I been followed the whole time, as Druett had warned me might be the case? Had Scantbury told his tale and named me as the abductor – in which event, was I to be arrested? It looked, I realised, as if someone was still working to remove all traces of the failed Anniversary Plot, to the extent of eliminating anyone who knew of it.

I spent an hour or more in this condition of mind, looking out of the window at times, alternately sitting or pacing the room. The old man, far from being troubled by my restlessness, ignored me until I at last realised he was asleep, head slumped and hands dangling between his knees; how he did not fall to the floor was a minor miracle. Not wanting to wake him, I was seating myself again when I heard the door latch, and footsteps on the threshold. On my feet, I turned to face the man who walked in, and who was undoubtedly John Baggot. Stopping in his stride, he gazed at me in surprise.

'You're the one who hired Oldrigg.'

'I am,' I said. 'How did you know it?'

'I saw you through the window, when you came before.' He eyed me warily - and I observed yet another ex-soldier, heavy-jowled and rough-bearded, with what looked like a powder burn covering a part of one cheek. London seemed full of these veterans, the jetsam of the King's Peace... at which moment, the man's father awoke and looked round.

'You've small need to wonder who this gentleman's come looking for,' he said sourly. 'Best tell him what you know, and have done with it.'

There was a short silence, in which I understood something else. It was a brief movement, yet it told me enough: instinctively Baggot's hand went to his neck, before he lowered it hurriedly. There was a crucifix under his old soldier's coat; like his lodger, of course, he was a papist. The man's eyes met mine, and he saw that I knew.

'Where is Oldrigg?' I demanded, having no desire to waste more time.

'I don't know – I swear it,' he answered.

'When was he here last?'

'This morning... I haven't seen him all day.'

'Has anyone else been here, asking for him?'

'Not that I've seen...' the man was growing resentful. 'And who are you to question me in this manner?'

'I'm a former magistrate,' I told him. 'And since I believe a felony may have been committed, I need whatever intelligence you can give me. Or I'm minded to return with pursuivants and search your house.'

There was a grunt from behind me, followed by a muffled oath; the old man was getting unsteadily to his feet. In agitation, he levelled a finger at his son.

'I told you it would come to this,' he accused. 'As I told you not to take that fellow in – did I not say he'd bring trouble on us?'

'Hold your peace,' John Baggot said, though without anger. To me he said: 'I'm not Oldrigg's keeper, nor do I meddle in his affairs. I took him in a few weeks back because he was close to vagrancy... he even owes me rent. Whatever he's done, I'll swear I've no part in it.'

'Tell him what that man is - what he was.' The older Baggot said angrily. 'For if you don't, I will,' he added with a glance at me. 'We're not at fault here – our only shame is giving shelter to a...'

'A what – a papist militant?' I broke in; on a sudden, matters were beginning to make sense. 'For I already know that Oldrigg fought not for the Crown, but for its enemy – I mean the Spanish Regiment. He confided in me, of his own free will.'

Father and son looked at each other; neither spoke, for there was no need. Oldrigg, we all knew, had gone to Flanders to serve the regiment of disaffected souls who fought against their fellow countrymen, for the Catholic cause. After the treaty with Spain he too had returned home - but unlike men like Richard Elms, in denial of his true allegiance. In which case... I looked hard at John Baggot, who at once shook his head.

'No - I did not fight for that party, if that's the way your mind moves,' he said firmly. 'I'm no traitor, despite what you may think. Yes, we're of the Roman faith as our family has always been - but we're loyal Englishmen for all that.'

He indicated the old man. 'My father fought for Queen Elizabeth's army once, in France,' he said. 'There's no shame in trailing a pike for your country. I was a cannoneer, and have the marks to testify to it...' this, with a hand to the blue-black mark on his cheek. 'Most of us obey our superiors, and forbear to take up arms against our own country. Hence you do me an injustice, sir, to bracket me with a man like Oldrigg, who believed otherwise and fought according to his conscience. You may condemn him for it, yet…' He paused. 'Yet, even though he and I fought on different sides, I cannot.'

I was silent. By the fireside, the old man sank down heavily on his stool, averting his gaze. John Baggot hesitated, then went over to sit facing him. After a while he looked up and gestured to another stool.

'Sit if you will, and I'll tell what I can of Oldrigg, though it's precious little,' he said. But being anxious to take my leave now, I refused.

'All I want is to find him,' I told him. 'I have no quarrel with you – but if you press me, I'll return with a warrant for your arrest for housing a traitor.'

'I've told you already, I don't know where he is,' Baggot threw back.

'Not even a suspicion?' I persisted. 'See now, loyalty is a virtue, but this is a grave matter. I might even say, there are lives at stake.'

Both men looked at me: the younger in some irritation, the older in alarm.

'What do you mean?' The old man asked. 'What is it he's done?'

'He's taken someone by force,' I admitted, tired of evasion. 'Someone enfeebled, who may perish for lack of care. I won't tell more, but I have to know where they might be.'

'God's heart…' With an air of weariness, he turned to his son. 'Is this what we're brought to, by your misplaced charity? If you've any inkling where that rogue might go, then tell the gentleman.'

But the younger man merely drew a breath, met his gaze and said: 'I'll not turn informer on any man of my faith – not even on him.' And with arms folded he regarded me steadily, as if bidding me to do my worst.

So, it was no use; without a word I turned and left the house, watched in silence by both men. Thereafter it was a miserable walk back to Druett's, with the weight of failure upon me: the knowledge that all my efforts had now come to naught, and that Thomas Jessop would likely never be seen again.

Until, that is, I entered the house to find, if not uproar, then a good deal of activity - and came to an astonished halt. In the parlour was Oldrigg, looking tired and dishevelled - and by the fire sat a huddled figure wrapped in a blanket.

It was Thomas.

Well now: what a night that was, of confession and more. From being enraged with Oldrigg for his treachery, I was now almost bereft of speech. The sight of Thomas Jessop safe and unharmed, as well as that of John and Francis Druett who had given him shelter, drove my anger and despondency away, and I was most grateful for a chair and a cup of sack to restore me. Thereafter, Thomas being too wearied to talk much, he was got to bed by the servants. Frances too retired, by which time I had recovered my wits enough to demand an explanation from Oldrigg – who confounded me by going on the attack.

'You should have told me more about Philip, Master Belstrang – or can I call him Thomas now?' He said. 'You'd no cause to distrust me, merely on account of my faith.'

Having no ready answer, I was silent. Druett, sitting beside me, wore his lawyer's face.

'I've been watched, it seems,' my one-time servant went on, 'likely since I entered your service - and soon after I left you at the glass-painter's, they pounced.'

'Who did?' Druett asked sharply.

'Men-at-arms, pursuivants – call them what you like, they're all the same to me. They knew who I was – and they knew how to bend me to their will.'

I frowned; a change had come over the man – an expression I had never seen before: to my surprise, it looked like fear.

'I was given a simple choice,' he went on. 'Wait a while, then go back to the Biershaws and bring Thomas away from them. I could tell them whatever tale I liked - but if I left there without him, the price would be more than I could refuse. After that I was to move him to somewhere private - and kill him.'

A moment followed, while Druett and I eyed each other.

'I told you Machyn would act,' Druett murmured. 'I'll wager all I have that this was on his orders.'

'This threat… this price you couldn't refuse,' I began, but Oldrigg forestalled me.

'You assume I meant money?' he demanded. 'Do you think so basely of me?'

'In God's name, I no longer know what to think,' I replied. 'You told the Biershaws I'd sent you, which was a lie, so how should I-'

'My family,' Oldrigg said harshly. 'Those men swore they would torture me until I broke, and told them where they are. Then they would kill every last one of them, down to the youngest. She's but two years old - and from the looks of them, they meant it!'

'By the Christ,' Druett said, with a shake of his head; while I could only watch Oldrigg, who was close to despair.

'I had no notion you had a family,' I said at last.

'I thought they were safe…they're with friends of our faith. I was trying to get enough money together, to get them out of this country…' he looked up. 'And they're in peril yet, as long as Jessop's still alive,' he said in anguish. 'Now do you see what you've done?'

'Well, I believe I do,' I said after a moment; a chill had stolen over my heart. 'Though I dearly hope it's not too late to save them, and you.' I looked at Druett, but to my surprise he held up a hand. Stony-faced, he eyed Oldrigg.

'And yet, with that terrible threat hanging over you, you let the young man live,' he said without emotion. 'Why, pray, did you do that?'

We waited, he and I. Oldrigg looked at each of us in turn, gave a great sigh and spread his hands.

'How could I not spare him?' He said. 'Once he'd told me his tale… once I'd learned what he was willing to do for his faith, and how he'd been worked like a puppet by those curs - those devils, who used him so vilely? Because he was loyal and brave, and would have slain the Stuart viper in his lair as he deserves, save that he was duped, and almost lost his mind over it…' he shook his head.

'Think what you will of me, sirs,' he went on. 'I've been a soldier who's slain men in battle – yet as God is my witness, a murderer I am not! Now - in His holy name, what am I to do?'

NINETEEN

The morning following dawned fresh and fair - and despite all that had been said and done, it brought hope: hope not only for Oldrigg and his family, but for Thomas Jessop too. For there was one course open to us, it seemed, and one only: to get all of them safely out of England before it was too late.

At first Druett had been sceptical; he and I had risked enough, he argued, and the danger was far from past – in fact, it could now be greater than it was. Though Oldrigg had assured us both that he had not been followed since abducting Thomas from the Biershaws, nor when he had brought him to Druett's house under cover of darkness, my friend was unconvinced. And yet, turn it about as we did - for half the night, until all three of us were weary of it - a resolution of sorts had at last been reached. In short, Druett would provide a sum, which I would repay, to buy a passage by ship to France - not only for Thomas but for Oldrigg, and his wife and children. Once there, they could make their way to whatever safe destination they chose.

There was no other remedy; and now that Oldrigg's plight had been made clear, and once I saw how courageously he'd acted, I was eager to move matters on. It was not the outcome I had wished, let alone the one John Jessop wished for his son, but at least the youth's life would be saved. And indeed, when I roused Thomas in the morning and told him of our proposed solution, he was cheered more than I expected. He could go to Rome, he said, as he'd once dreamed... he might try to enter the priesthood. And he had only warmth and affection for Oldrigg – especially when he learned of the man's predicament, and the risks he had taken to save him. Thomas would be ready to travel soon, he vowed – even if he had to be trussed up in a sack and loaded on to a cart. Which indeed, was close enough to the facts.

The facts were these: *Primus*: Oldrigg would hire a cart, which he could drive; *Secundus*: with Thomas as his passenger – a sick young man, well-muffled, who was being taken to stay with relatives - he would leave at nightfall, drive to where his family stayed, and remove them from their hiding place; both Druett and I refrained from asking him where that was. Thereafter Oldrigg would lose no time in getting them all to the port of Deptford on the south bank of the Thames, where he had a contact who would hide them until a passage was found on a vessel leaving for France. After which, trusting to luck and the weather, another group of desperate Papists would sail out of the England of James Stuart, to freedom.

There remained, however, one difficulty: how to preserve the safety of the one who had brought all of this about: digging for facts, thwarting the will of those who had planned - and almost succeeded in carrying out - the Anniversary Plot, and who now wanted all knowledge of it erased; one who had avoided attempts not only on his own life, but on that of the duped assassin who yet lived to spill his tale. I speak, of course, of Robert Belstrang, former Justice of Worcestershire, and now a somewhat frightened man.

'I'm safe enough – or at least I hope so,' Druett said as we sat at breakfast. 'I could deny all knowledge of the whole business if I had to...' He eyed me grimly. 'Even if I have to deny aiding you.'

'You must,' I told him. 'I'll not have you and Frances harmed...'

'I doubt it'll come to that,' he broke in. 'I've told you I'm not without influence at Court - though I'll avoid Sir Roland Machyn in future. What we must do now is form a strategy, so that you can get yourself away and back to Thirldon.'

I lowered my gaze, moving porridge about with my spoon; at that moment I could have wept. It seemed like months since I was home... what Hester and Childers would be thinking of my extended absence, I could not imagine.

'I won't delay any longer,' I said. 'I already owe you so much... once I've seen Oldrigg drive Thomas out of the city I'll take the road for Uxbridge, and you'll be rid of me. And to the devil with anyone who tries to follow me – I may be old, but I believe my Leucippus can outrun any horse in London.'

He regarded me, then: 'I regret, old friend, that it may not be as simple.'

'I feared you might say so,' I admitted, after a moment. 'You think I'll be seen before I even reach the Temple Bars – and waylaid as soon as I reach Hounslow Heath, or some other lonely spot.'

Druett's silence was assent enough.

'What if I took a different route? Rode east, by twists and turns through the city to lose any pursuers, then crossed the Bridge and travelled through Surrey before striking the west road?'

'Perhaps – may we both think on it?' He rose, suddenly brisk and ready to go about his business. 'At least wait until tomorrow morning, after seeing Oldrigg and Jessop off. You'll need a night's rest before setting out.'

To that I agreed, and there was little more to say. With money from Druett -whose generosity we had prevailed on long enough - Oldrigg had gone to hire a cart, which he would bring to a quiet street nearby, before dusk. Thereafter I spent an anxious day, readying Leucippus for a long ride and getting my baggage packed. By late afternoon I was mighty restless, and only Frances's calmness sustained me.

'I'll not forget what you and John have done,' I told her. 'My hope is that one day you'll both come to Thirldon, and be my and Hester's honoured guests for as long as you like.'

To which she merely smiled, and said that it was her hope too.

Evening came at last, and all was ready. Thomas Jessop, rested but still very weak, was in borrowed clothes, while Oldrigg too had changed his attire. He had returned to the Baggot house to collect his belongings and make his peace with them: John Baggot was willing enough, though both he and his father were clearly relieved to their lodger go. But Oldrigg's thoughts were for his family now, and little else.

And in the end, the partings were brief and hurried. Druett and I rode with the cart as far as Cripplegate to see it leave the city; to everyone's relief, nobody appeared to be following. At the gate we made our farewells; Druett was cool towards both Oldrigg and Thomas. He could never excuse what Thomas had done, yet for my sake he would keep his silence. When both men thanked him with all their hearts, he nodded and drew back, whereupon I too took my leave.

'I pray you'll give my undying love to my mother and father, and beg their forgiveness for what I've brought upon them,' Thomas said to me, his voice somewhat shaky. 'Say I will write to them, when I'm safely overseas.' And when I assured him I would do so, the youth leaned towards me, put out a hand and grasped my arm.

''Whatever our differences in the matter of religion, sir, I'll hold you dearly in my heart for the rest of my days,' he said. He was close to tears, while I could do naught but nod and wish him well. Thereupon, I took farewell of Oldrigg.

'As I said once, you're a curious man,' he said as we shook hands; his grip could have crushed mine, had he chosen. 'Yet I wish I'd had you alongside me, in many a campaign... bless you, Master Belstrang.'

He turned and shook the reins; both the horses were restless, and eager to be moving. The cart rumbled away, past the Fore Street Conduit before turning left and out of our sight. Neither of its occupants looked back.

'When all's said and weighed, you've saved that young man's life – and helped to save an entire family too,' I said to Druett as we rode back. 'To me, it seems a grave injustice that you'll never receive any credit for it.'

But he made no answer; we did not speak again until suppertime, when it was a great relief to talk of everyday matters with Frances, and to try and put the last turbulent week behind us.

In the morning we rose early, ready for my departure - but it was not to be.

To everyone's alarm a visitor arrived, knocking loudly upon the door and asking for Master Justice Belstrang - and at sight of him I was astonished: it was George Bull.

'You must come with me, sir,' he said at once; he was out of sorts, clearly having ridden hard. 'We're summoned, you and I - and we cannot refuse.'

'How so?' I demanded. 'What on earth has occurred?'

'We're called to swear an oath,' George answered impatiently. 'There's a man at my house – a most unwelcome arrival, I might add. He's been there since soon after daybreak. I'm ordered to take you there - otherwise we'll both be arrested, he says. In God's name, sir, will you ready yourself and ride with me…?'

He broke off and turned to Druett, who had come into the hallway and was regarding him stonily; there was little warmth between these two.

'Summoned by whom, might I ask?' Druett enquired. But George was unwilling to answer, until I pressed him.

'As it happens, I am ready to ride – though I planned to do so in a different direction,' I said. 'If I'm to meet with this man, I insist on knowing who he is.'

To which George gave a sigh of exasperation. 'His name's Darby,' he said finally. 'He's a lawyer too – even if he's not one I'd deal with, if I had any choice in the matter. Yet I have no choice – and neither do you. So, for the sake of our family if nothing more, will you come?'

We rode in silence for most of the journey, northwards from the city through Islington to Highgate. I had learned nothing further from George since we set out, when he told me he had sent Anne and Kate to a neighbour's house while we conducted our business; a business which seemed as distasteful to him as it did to me. All I knew of this man Darby was what Druett had told me already, and had embellished in haste as I took horse: that he was a harsh and choleric fellow, as unyielding as he was corrupt – and hence, that everything he said should be doubted. However, there was another matter that rankled with me, and which was now uppermost in my mind: that this was the man to whom Druett had been obliged to settle the bogus debt which landed me in the Compter. Now the memory was raked up again, to say that I was angry would be short of the mark: in truth, I would happily have sworn out a warrant myself against Darby and seen him thrown into prison in his turn – without any means of escape.

When we reached George's house all was quiet, a wisp of

smoke from a chimney being the only sign of life. But as we dismounted, and a servant came out to take the reins, the man bent close and spoke to his master.

'He's in your private parlour, sir, making himself as comfortable as you please... you might think he had rights to the place.'

George and I exchanged looks, before entering the house and walking directly to his room. The door was ajar, but George threw it wide; he was controlling himself with difficulty. I followed him inside, to see a balding man in a lawyer's gown, standing with his back to us. At once he turned around, in his hand a book which he had clearly taken from the shelf behind him.

'Here you are at last, Bull,' he said in a bland tone. 'I grew bored, so I took the liberty of perusing your *Justinian*... a splendidly-bound copy.'

'I hope you found it enlightening,' George replied. 'I expect it's a while since you looked into the finer points of law.'

We all regarded each other in silence: George and I as taut as guy-ropes, the other man seemingly unconcerned – yet his chest rose and fell rapidly, betraying a turbulent temperament within. This, I felt certain, was one who served Sir Roland Machyn, if not others too: the one who dirtied his hands, enabling men like Machyn to keep their distance. I saw a ruddy-faced, heavy man of middle years, with a reddish beard trimmed to a dagger-point, and the eyes of a thief.

'Shall we sit?' Darby said, glancing towards a table.

'You may, if you like,' George told him. 'I prefer to stand.'

'As do I,' I said, to which Darby barely shrugged. Seating himself, he indicated a document which was spread out before him.

'I trust Bull has acquainted you with the agreement I'm instructed to obtain,' he said, eyeing me without expression. 'I need only your signature – both your signatures – and then I'll be on my way. I'm a busy man, and have clients waiting.'

There was a brief silence, before George spoke.

'His demands are similar to those conveyed to us by Sir Roland Machyn, though in more formal terms,' he said, turning to me. 'In short, you and I, Master Justice, are to swear never to reveal any inkling of the matter you uncovered—'

'Uncovered?' Darby broke in sharply. 'You misunderstand, Bull. There was no matter to uncover, for it never existed. No conspiracies, no talk of planned attempts on His Majesty's life, real or imagined...' He turned his gaze upon me. 'Failure to swear to that would result in the most serious consequences for you, Belstrang. Your house and land confiscated, and a heavy fine imposed – more than you are able to pay, I promise. Failure to settle, of course, would result in your being sent directly to the Fleet Prison for debts unpaid.'

'The Fleet?' I enquired, controlling my temper with difficulty. 'Why not the Compter, where I was once before?'

'The Fleet,' Darby repeated irritably. 'Where I believe you'll find the warders somewhat harder to bribe – not that you'll have the means, in any case.'

We eyed each other. Beside me, I sensed George's fear that I would lose my control and say something rash... he opened his mouth, but I stayed him.

'It's been some years since I sat at the bench myself, sir,' I said to Darby. 'Would you care to remind me what the penalty is for swearing out false warrant against a gentleman for a debt that never existed, then taking payment for the afore-mentioned debt? I would be most interested.'

'I appear to have forgotten,' Darby answered at once. 'But it scarcely matters: there's no record of any such warrant, nor any such debt, nor any mention of you in the prison books, sir. I trust that clarifies the matter.'

I drew a breath; in my mind's eye I saw the two stone-faced turnkeys in the Counter, demanding their admittance fee before writing my name down. I saw the bloated figure of Cotfield demanding my last coin, before shoving me into that cold and stinking room with its sick inhabitants. I saw the smug look on his features when he demanded my shoes along with my belt, before he would deliver my message at his own pace...

'In point of fact, it doesn't,' I said then, prompting George to give a start. 'Supposing, for example, I was to call certain witnesses to attest to my presence in the Compter – including a gentleman of repute, who conversed with me there?'

'Do you mean Curriter?' Darby snapped. A sneer appeared. 'Alas, the poor man's an inveterate gambler - got himself imprisoned again within days of his release, I understand. I somehow doubt he'll walk free again.'

Despite my best efforts my gorge rose, and I felt my cheeks burn. 'Nothing left to chance, then?' I said, somewhat bitterly.

'I've no notion what you mean,' the other replied. 'Now, may we cease wasting time? If you'll both sign the paper, our business is complete.'

I glanced at George, who hesitated - and more than before I pitied him, understanding his predicament only too well. Though an honest man, his thoughts were for Anne and their daughter - for their safety and livelihood, as well as his own reputation. Whereas this man who threatened him so shamelessly - this hard-hearted envoy of those who wished all traces of the Anniversary Plot erased, and would use any means to secure it - made my flesh crawl; I even felt a brief urge to reach for my sword.

But we were trapped, both George and I. With sinking heart, I weighed up the chances of avoiding signing the paper and realised they were nil... whereupon a notion sprang up.

'Who will stand witness to our signatures, then?' I enquired, looking round. 'There doesn't appear to be anyone else present.'

'Don't trouble yourself about that,' Darby said, impatient again. 'I will deal with matters of ratification later...'

'Indeed?' To my surprise, George spoke up sharply. 'As a lawyer, I'm loth to permit such – nor should you request it, sir. I fear the Chief Justice, should he learn of this, would be displeased – not to say suspicious.' He paused, then: 'I speak of Sir Edward Coke, whom I sought out only two days ago. I saw Machyn instead - but I would not allow myself to be diverted like that again. In short...'

'In short?' Darby broke in, with a most unpleasant twist of his mouth. 'What in heaven's name do you expect to achieve by this, Bull?'

To which George hesitated – but it was all I needed. The

notion I'd just had was growing into something clearer, perhaps even hopeful; taking a step towards the table, which caused Darby to flinch, I leaned over him.

'See now, did Sir Roland not brief you in full?' I asked, raising my eyebrows. 'Did he make no mention of the sworn deposition I made, setting out every detail of my investigations of the Plot you wish to make disappear – copies of it to be sent in person to Sir Edward and to His Majesty, and also to both Secretaries of State?'

And when Darby made no answer, I placed my hands flat on the table. 'Come sir,' I went on. 'Did you think me so foolish as to take no steps to protect myself?'

'You bluff, Belstrang,' came the reply. 'I would know of such, and besides-'

He trailed off, but he was flustered, as if he'd been about to let something slip – and seizing the moment, I went on the attack.

'Are you certain of that?' I demanded. 'What if I told you what I told Sir Roland, even if he disbelieved me: that a servant of mine has in his possession a full report of my investigations, with orders to take it to Sir Thomas Lake if anything happens to me?'

Flushed and angry, Darby stood up suddenly – far too quickly, in fact, for a man of his physique and temperament.

'How dare you speak to me like this!' he shouted, pointing a finger. 'You think to threaten me, who serves the highest in the kingdom? I could have you hanged, Belstrang - more, to the devil with a trial: I could have you disappear this very night, your body not found until only the bones are left! I'm giving you a chance to forget this entire business – this foolish tale you've fixed in your mind - and to go away free! Are you truly so simple as to refuse – refuse one who serves not only Machyn, but-'

He stopped. There was an odd look on his face... then came uncertainty. To the surprise of both George and I, Darby swayed slightly where he stood, then fell back into the chair he'd vacated. As we watched, he put a hand to his chest.

'It's but a flux,' he muttered, looking up at me, then at George. 'It comes at times, but it will elapse when I rest and take some physic...' he winced, as the pain worsened. 'Strong water is usually enough... and warmth... I pray you...'

'You do what?' I demanded, with a swift look at George. 'You expect us to aid you until you're restored, and ready to bind us both to this testament – this web of lies? Do you truly think we would do so?'

And when doubt clouded Darby's features, I allowed myself a smile.

'No, sir,' I said. 'What I propose to do is to take you outside, put you on my horse and take you to a physician, as any Christian man would do to help one in such a case. Of course, it may take a while to find one, since I'm unfamiliar with the area, and during which time your condition may worsen - but I'm merely an ex-magistrate, and no Doctor of Physic. How terrible it would be then, if you slipped into unconsciousness and had to be set down by the roadside... how people would gather and gape, while I urged them to give you air... what, are you dismayed?' I asked, seeing the look on his face. 'Well then, what would you have us do – could we not perhaps, come to some agreement?'

To which the man made no answer, but gave what sounded like a moan; with a look of concern, I bent closer.

'I didn't hear that,' I said. 'Did you, George?'

I turned and gave him a long look, to which he at first made no reply, then: 'I don't believe I did, sir,' he said quietly.

Whereupon, we waited.

TWENTY

He lay on a made-up pallet on the floor of George's main parlour, close to the fireside and covered with a blanket. Servants had brought a strong draught, a herbal brew of Anne's, learned long ago from her mother. After drinking it and resting a while, Darby was recovered enough to talk – but whatever notions he harboured of compromise were soon dashed. For it took me only a short time to assure him that, even if no report of the kind I'd described to him existed, he could be certain that it would very soon – and his part in the business would not be omitted. Once that was understood, his manner altered considerably.

'Surely you can see I'm but the messenger – the facilitator?' He demanded; his face was pale, and sheened with sweat. 'I draw up papers, nothing more - I'm a lawyer for hire, like you.'

He addressed himself to George, but by now George's manner had altered too.

'You're not like me, Darby,' he said. 'You've taken me for a fool – or a milksop, perhaps. But I know the law as well as you, as I know Sir Edward Coke, who tried the Powder Plotters - you can guess how he would view this wicked business. It's you who may find your house confiscated, your family left destitute… you do have a family, I seem to recall?'

Darby looked away, and said nothing.

'Well then,' I said brightly, my spirits having lifted a good deal. 'Before you leave us, perhaps we could – as I said some time ago – come to an agreement? None need know of it save the three of us… do you see?'

I sat on a chair, consoled by a cup of George's claret, while George himself paced the room. His distaste was still evident, but he was a good deal calmer than when he had arrived at Druett's early that morning. He stopped and looked down at his unwelcome guest, who returned his gaze.

'What manner of agreement?' Darby asked, with a sickly look in my direction.

'I see a way forward,' I told him, 'which would mean drawing up another contract, somewhat different to the one you were so eager for us to sign – which contract,' I added, 'we could still sign, thereby letting you off the hook. In short, you may return to your masters, having obtained what they wanted, and there the matter would end - as far as they're aware.'

'Are you serious, sir?'

George was frowning at me. 'Do you truly intend to sign that... that pack of lies, despite all you've said?'

'I do,' I said, 'and for all your principles, George, I urge you to sign it too. For by doing so, we'll both be free to go about our business.'

At that his consternation increased, whereupon I bade him sit down; by now I'd compassed the way out for us both, and was determined to follow it through.

'As I said, once we've signed Darby's paper, we've done what's demanded of us,' I told him. 'The existence, however, of another sworn statement would be known only to those of us in this room: one outlining my findings as to the intended plot against the King, and all that has since followed. Darby would then append his signature, affirming that he knew of it, and took steps to have the matter suppressed. He would therefore be guilty by association - or even, I suggest, an accessory to the plot, since mere knowledge of such an activity could amount to treason.' I faced Darby. 'Do you wish to correct me on that point?'

Again, the man had no answer - but a fearful look had come over him.

'Furthermore,' I went on, 'I will, of course, have copies made of our document. One would remain with Bull, another would be lodged with my lawyers, and you would have another. But there would also be a fourth copy, deposited in a location known only to myself. Should anything untoward happen to me or any of my family, the person holding the paper would be under instruction to make it public.'

'And if I refuse to sign your damned paper?' Darby asked, after a pause.

'Then neither Master Bull nor I will sign yours. You'll have failed – and more, my report would be sent at once to The Chief Justice. I doubt you're fit to ride yet… it's only a matter of common charity, that we keep you here and look after you for the present.'

Darby let out a long sigh. 'To the devil with you, Belstrang,' he said, with a shake of his head.

'I might reply in the same manner, after what you put me through,' I retorted. 'I assume it was on Machyn's orders, as was the killing of Edmund Anstis – and the entrapment of Thomas Je-' I stopped myself, having almost blurted out a name I meant to conceal. I was growing most heated, and drew a calming breath.

'What a posse of rogues there are in Whitehall nowadays,' I finished.

'Enough, damn you!'

On a sudden, Darby was agitated. Throwing aside the blanket, he got somewhat shakily to his feet. 'Let me sit, for pity's sake,' he said to George. 'I can do you no harm, can I?'

A chair was brought and placed a short distance away. Darby sat down heavily and eyed us both, then after a while he spoke.

'It's not Machyn you should fear,' he said quietly.

'Indeed?' I frowned at him – whereupon George spoke up sharply.

'What - is it his master, then?' he demanded.

Darby made no answer, while George and I exchanged looks: surely not the joint Secretary of State…?

'You mean Winwood? Sir Ralph Winwood himself?' I asked.

Darby looked away – and in moment George was on his feet again.

'By God, I see it,' he said - and at last, I began to see it too.

'We've been blind,' George went on. 'As blind as Thomas Jessop. We should have thought of who would be blamed, after the plot succeeded: the papists, and-'

'Stop!' Darby cried. 'You fool - have you still not grasped it? The Anniversary Plot was never supposed to succeed – it was intended to fail!'

We gazed at him. My mind was busy… in truth, I was overwhelmed.

'Tell us, here and now,' I said. 'Or by the Christ, I'll…' I stopped, fearing my anger would get the better of me.

'What… what will you do?' Darby asked, eying me bleakly. 'What can any of us do, who haven't the ear of the King, as others have?'

I fell silent. After a moment George sat down again; he looked more than astonished - he looked spent. So, for that matter, did Darby… and since there was little use in lying now, he spoke up.

'Thomas Jessop was a hapless dupe, but he was never meant to kill the King,' he said tiredly. 'He was to be overpowered before he could get close enough, then slain before he could talk – so the King's rescuer could take credit for saving His Majesty's life. It really was as simple as that.'

'And his rescuer,' I began –

'Would be Winwood, of course,' Darby snapped. 'The hero of the hour.'

'Well… indeed,' George put in, his mouth taut. 'And as I was going to say, the Papists would be blamed for hatching the plot: the Percys and Montagues, pro-Catholics like the Seymours and Herberts, the Countess of Shrewsbury - and of course, Sir Thomas Lake… good God!'

He stared at me. 'This is a tale of two courtiers who loathe each other – rivals for the King's favour!'

We both turned to Darby, who regarded us sourly.

'You could do better than merely pen a report,' he said bitterly. 'Perhaps you should make a play of it.'

Whereupon, like a beam of light, the last element of the puzzle flew up before me.

'Sarmiento… the ambassador,' I said. 'He too would be suspect, and hence expelled, whereupon the Spanish Match-'

'Would be dead in the water,' George finished. 'And aside from men like me, who desires that most of all? Winwood, who knew Anstis in the Hague, and knew he could bribe him - while to all appearances he served Sir Thomas Lake.'

'Indeed.' I nodded to him. 'The Secretary who was losing

favour, jealous of Lake and angry with the King for his prodigal ways, not to say his intentions regarding the Match... by this means he could teach him a lesson, smear the papists and endear himself to His Majesty - in one swoop.'

'That fool of a Stuart.'

It was Darby who spoke, without looking at either of us. 'Such glorious ambition,' he muttered, as if to himself. 'With his daughter now married to the Prince of Bohemia, and with a son married to the daughter of the Spanish King, he would be the power broker of Europe – or so he thought. Rex Pacificus? Nay, Rex Magnificus! The nearest thing to a God he could get... and all for vanity. I curse his very soul.'

'As might others, if this ever came out,' I murmured.

'So - you know the whole of it,' Darby sighed. 'Now are you content?'

George said nothing; he was still shaken. Hence, it was I who brought things to a conclusion.

'Just now, only one thing would content me,' I answered, gathering my scattered wits. 'Your signature on the paper I will draw up. So - shall we to business?'

At supper that night, feeling a good deal calmer, I sat while George told Anne all that had passed, rendering her speechless. Finally, when there was nothing further to add, I rose with cup in hand and offered a toast to them both.

'And I wish to exact a promise from you,' I said. 'That you will bring Kate, and come to spend Yuletide with us at Thirldon this year. May I have it on oath?'

I looked to George, who nodded. 'With all my heart, Master Justice,' he said, while Anne's smile was answer enough. As I sat down again, even the thought of winter cheered me: the looming end to my Year of Astonishment.

'You'll spend the night here?' George said, breaking my reverie, though it was hardly a question. 'And on the morrow...'

'On the morrow I must take my leave of you all, quite early,' I said, 'for I've much to do.' I raised my eyebrows to my son-in-law. 'As I expect, have you.'

'I do,' he answered. 'Though it's petty stuff - a land dispute between neighbours. Nothing grand...' he allowed himself a smile. 'And yet, I might try to catch up with the gossip. I believe I'll be taking a closer interest in matters of state, in the future.'

'I think you should,' I said. 'There's a need for men who care about England's future, without seeking merely to serve their own ends.'

Whereupon I felt a yawn coming on, and said I would go to my bed.

When I brought Leucippus round from Druett's stable, John and Catherine stood at their door to send me on my way. There was little left to say after I'd told them what had transpired, and how it had ended with Samuel Darby's sullen departure the previous afternoon. He carried our agreement, signed and witnessed by George's servants, and had viewed the rough copy I'd made, ready to be recopied. Despite his loss of face, he was unrepentant; men like him would never change. He could take his master the false document, and show that all had been done as ordered. For the record, no tenth Anniversary Plot of the 5th of November 1615 had ever been planned, or even conceived: it was merely the fiction of a young man of diseased mind, who had since disappeared and was presumed dead.

'What will you tell Jessop's father?' Druett asked, as I took my leave.

'That his son is safe,' I said. 'That, I think, should be enough.'

I embraced Catherine: a warm clasping, from which I broke away quickly. John and I shook hands, and I gripped his shoulder.

'I'll send money as soon as I'm home – all that I owe you, and more,' I said. 'I would ask that a sum be given to Biershaw the glass-painter and his family... can you arrange that?'

He nodded, and now at last all was done. I looked up: the day was fair again, and the ride would be good for both Leucippus and myself. I got myself mounted, bade them farewell, then rode off down Coleman Street; I had no wish to look back.

At the junction with Lothbury I reined in. I could turn left, as Druett had advised, and make my way eastwards to

Bishopsgate, thence to the Bridge and over into Surrey; or I could turn right and make for Ludgate, where I had first entered London more than a fortnight since. After all, I was a free man now - was I not?

And yet, with a new-found caution that I believe I will take to my grave, I shook the reins and went left.